So You Want To Start A House Church?

OTHER BOOKS BY FRANK VIOLA

Volume 2: Who is Your Covering?
A Fresh Look at Leadership, Authority, and Accountability

Volume 3: Pagan Christianity:
The Origins of Our Modern Church Practices

Volume 4: So You Want to Start a House Church?
First-Century Styled Church Planting For Today

Volume 5: From Nazareth to Patmos:
The Saga of the New Testament Church

Straight Talk to Elders

Knowing Christ Togther

The Untold Story of the New Testament Church

**Visit the Present Testimony Ministry Web Site for
Free Downloads and Ordering Information:**

www.ptmin.org

SO YOU WANT TO START
A HOUSE CHURCH?

*First-Century Styled
Church Planting For Today*

Frank Viola

To all church planters of the past who counted the cost, forged the path, and showed the way . . . and to a future generation of young men and women called of God who will stand on their shoulders and see farther than they did.

CONTENTS

Section 1:
First-Century Principles of Church Planting

Section 2:
Objections and Responses

FOREWORD

There is a growing "church-in-the-home" movement across the United States and around the world. Frank Viola is one of many that God is using to trumpet the call to return to meeting in homes.

I have never had the privilege of meeting Frank Viola. But I have been greatly blessed by His writings.

The most effective way to evangelize the world—and disciple converts—is the planting of simple, Biblical churches. This was the pattern throughout the New Testament. The churches that the early apostles planted were simple churches that met in the homes of the believers: *House churches!*

In recent years much has been written about church planting, but usually in the context of planting traditional churches. And much has been written about the emerging apostolic ministry, but again in the context of the apostolic ministry functioning in the traditional church setting. Much has been written about "house church," but not much has been written about house church planting.

That is what this book is all about—the New Testament ministry of planting house churches. The author looks at four different ways that churches came into existence in the first century. He also speaks on the subject of how church planters were trained and how they conducted their ministries.

Many "church-in-the-home" groups have a sense that they are not experiencing all that God has for them. But they are not sure what to do about it. Some are beginning to sense that they should be multiplying—planting other churches—but are not sure what to do about it. You will find this book to be of great help. This book is very Christ-centered. It is all about extending the kingdom of Jesus Christ.

While you may not agree with every detail in this book, you will be greatly encouraged and instructed by reading it.

I have learned much from reading the manuscript. I wish I could have had it forty years ago when I first saw that God wanted to do something radical in His church.

Therefore, I predict that *So You Want to Start a House Church?* will be greatly used throughout the world. I hope and pray that it will.

Nate Krupp
Salem, Oregon

ACKNOWLEDGMENTS

After eight years of traversing the gamut of denominational, non-denominational, and para-church assemblies, I took the terrifying step of leaving the institutional church. Upon leaving, I found myself thrown headlong in the midst of a spontaneous expression of church life. That spontaneous expression lasted eight long years. Early into that experience, I was exposed to the way that churches were planted in the first century.

It all began when I was handed Watchman Nee's classic work *The Normal Christian Church Life*. In this book, Nee argues powerfully for the notion that virtually all churches in Century One were planted by extra-local workers. The book was the first to make a tremendous imprint on the way I understood church formation. I later came across Roland Allen's earlier volume, *Missionary Methods: St. Paul's or Ours?* Allen makes many of the same points that Nee made, but he uses different language.

Sometime after reading Allen, I was introduced to the scholarship of F.F. Bruce. To my mind, Bruce has no peer in understanding first-century church history and Paul's life and mission. In fact, if one weaves together all of Bruce's work on the first-century church, they will have the complete history of Paul's method of church planting.[1]

---

[1] Among his best are *Paul: The Apostle of the Heart Set Free, The Book of the Acts (Revised), In the Steps of Paul, New Testament History, Paul and His Converts, The Pauline Circle,* and *The Letters of Paul: An Expanded Translation.*

Other men have written on the subject since Nee, Allen, and Bruce. Most notably are my friends Rob Banks and Gene Edwards. Banks gives scholarly attention to the Pauline way of raising up churches in his book *Paul's Idea of Community (Chapters 15-18)*. And Edwards has written a raft of books tracing this principle throughout the NT (New Testament). His best known being the *First-Century Diaries* (a series of five books telling the story of the first-century church in novel form) and *How to Meet in Homes*.

Of all the men I have mentioned, Gene Edwards has broken the most ground in the area of primitive church planting. He has dedicated his entire adult life to restoring first-century principles for raising up churches as well as training Christian workers, and I have been privileged to participate in and benefit from this restoration.

My debt to Gene's fathering leadership is immense. May God raise up scores of spiritual fathers like him whose passion for the Lord Jesus, revolutionary spirit, and pioneering foresight encourages other young men to grow mighty in the grace of God. This book, therefore, owes a great deal to Gene Edwards, Rob Banks, F.F. Bruce, Roland Allen, and Watchman Nee. Special thanks also goes to Mike Biggerstaff and Howard Snyder for proofing the manuscript.

PREFACE

The principles set forth in this book are not untested theories. Unlike most books on church planting, you will not find arm-chair philosophy or bloodless abstractions within its pages. Neither will you find any hype or hoopla about a coming "apostolic wave" where God is going to raise up "thousands of apostles" at some elusive date set off in the unseen future.

Rather, the principles described in this book have been hammered out on the anvil of experience. There are church planters, past and present, that have fleshed them out. In addition, these principles are for *today*. They apply to *this* day and *this* hour. They are also supported by the voice of Scripture and the weight of NT scholarship.

Since I have been a Christian, I have made a number of observations regarding the problems endemic to the modern church—both institutional and house church. All of these experiences led me to the following conclusions:

1. Most modern churches, including the majority of house churches, have strayed far afield from the experience of the first-century church. The chief reason being that we have utterly ignored what Scripture has to say about God's way of planting churches.

2. Many of the problems germane to modern house churches could be resolved if we returned to first-century principles of church planting and nurturing.

Granted, these conclusions are built on pragmatic observations. But they also carry the force of Scripture to support them, and they are the seedbed that provoked this book.

Three books precede this one in a series on radical church reform. *Pagan Christianity* traces the origins of every modern church practice, showing that the institutional church does not have a historical right to exist. *Rethinking the Wineskin* and *Who is Your Covering?* compare the modern church to the NT church.[2] Both books present a living color image of first-century church life. To put it metaphorically, they give a detailed portrait of a very special woman.[3] They describe her appearance, her personality, her passion, and the unique way she expresses herself.

The book you hold in your hands picks up where *Rethinking* and *Covering* leave off. It seeks to take a snapshot look at how this woman is born and how God intends for her to grow.

Tragically, many modern Christians have the benighted idea that beginning a NT-styled church is like assembling *Lego* blocks. One simply has to stick their nose in the Bible, extract from its pages the practices of the early church, imitate them, and voilá, a floatable "NT church" is created.

But this way of thinking is profoundly flawed. A NT-styled church cannot be started by the bare hands of men—no more than a woman can be constructed through human ingenuity or

---

[2] It should be noted that I am using the word "church" throughout this volume as it is used in the NT. "Church" is not a building, a denomination, or a religious service. Rather, "church"—translated from the Greek word *ekklesia*—embodies two ideas: *Community* and *assembly*. The NT envisions the church as a close-knit *community* whose members share God's life and who *assemble* together regularly.

[3] I speak of the church (2 Cor. 11:2; Eph. 5:23-32).

imitation. A woman must be given birth. And once born, she must be nurtured to the point where she develops on her own.

Forgive the crass illustration, but lashing together two female arms and legs onto a torso and propping a female head on top will never produce a girl. To the naked eye such a concoction may resemble a human being. But it will always lack the essential quality of humanness—*life*. And life is the product of birth. This principle holds true when we consider "starting" an authentic church.

I have written this book for three different audiences.

First, it is written to the scores of people who desire to return to a first-century expression of church life.

Second, it is written to those who have set out to start a house church and have been unhappy with the results.

Third, it is written to every person—including pastors, missionaries, and house church leaders—who feels called to plant churches.   .

The purpose of this book is quite simple: To provide a survey of how churches were planted in the first century. And to show that the first-century way of planting churches is directly related to God's eternal purpose.

It is my contention that most Christians are stuck in the prevailing paradigms that dominate the Christian world today.[4] Accordingly, they have been blinded to God's highest intention. Let me illustrate with a historical example.

In the mid-20th century, Swiss watchmakers had the corner on the world market share of watches. But that changed when one of their own countrymen came out with a revolutionary new idea: The quartz watch. He presented this idea to the Swiss manufacturers and they laughed at him. They con-

---

[4] A paradigm is the overall understanding or model that is accepted by an intellectual community. A paradigm shift refers to a drastic change in that understanding or model.

cluded it could never work, so they refused to patent the idea. Seiko, on the other hand, took one look at the quartz watch and the rest is history.

The power of a paradigm had so influenced the Swiss watch manufacturers that they could not understand the new concept of the quartz watch. Because the quartz watch had no gears, no mainspring, and no bearings, they rejected it. Their present paradigm did not allow for the new innovation. The net effect was that they lost the leading edge on watchmaking and they were forced to lay off thousands of workers. It was all because the quartz watch did not fit into their world view. It did not fit within their paradigm. They did not appreciate the new way because they were blinded by the old way.

In the same way, a paradigm shift concerning the practice of the church *and* church planting is needed if the Body of Christ will be restored to her pristine glory. Note that a recovery of both church *practice* and church *planting* are needed. Both elements must be kept together.

The principles outlined in this book cannot be adapted to the present-day practice of the church. Modern church practice has few points of contact with the NT church. Thus using Biblical principles to plant institutional churches or to renew dead churches is futile. (It is far easier to have new born babies than to raise the dead!)

If our understanding of the church remains institutional, we are in danger of merely transplanting the prevailing church model that is characterized by top-down leadership and a passive laity. To do so is to perpetuate a defective ec-clesiology. In the same way, using modern institutional methods to plant NT-styled churches is a study in foolishness. It simply will not work. Sophisticated methods, even if they are built on ageless principles, cannot offset a contaminated system.

What is needed is a recovery of first-century styled church planting principles *to produce* first-century styled churches. Put another way, an entirely new paradigm must be embraced for both church practice and church planting. As Roland Allen puts it,

Men have wandered over the world, "preaching the Word," laying no solid foundations, establishing nothing permanent, leaving no really instructed society behind them, and have claimed St. Paul's authority for their absurdities . . . people have adopted fragments of St. Paul's method and have tried to incorporate them into alien systems, and the failure which resulted has been used as an argument against the Apostle's method . . . unless we are prepared to drag down St. Paul from his high position as the great Apostle of the Gentiles, we must allow his methods a certain character of universality, and now I venture to urge that, since the Apostle, no other has discovered or practiced methods for the propagation of the gospel better than his or more suitable to the circumstances of our day. It would be difficult to find any better model than the Apostle in the work of establishing new churches. At any rate this much is certain, that the Apostle's methods succeeded exactly where ours have failed. (Missionary Methods: St. Paul's or Ours?)

The rediscovery of the NT approach to church planting is an explosive that has the power to break traditional thinking and demolish institutional practice. For this reason, may you open your heart to behold a new way—which is really an ancient way—handcrafted by God Himself.

Frank Viola
Jacksonville, Florida
July 2003

INTRODUCTION

God's ultimate intention is to increase and express His Son so that He might fill all things. Throughout the NT, this intention is called "the mystery" or "the eternal purpose" (Eph. 1:9-12; 3:3-11; 5:25-32; Col. 1:25-2:3; Rev. 10:7).

From the Father's perspective, every time a church is born, His Son is increased and expressed. This is why the book of Acts tells us that when people came to Christ, they were added to "the church" as well as "added to the Lord" (Acts 2:47; 5:14; 11:24b). As the church grows, Christ grows. With each new person that is added to the church, a member is attached to Christ's Body.

While Jesus Christ is certainly distinct from His church, He is not separate from it. He is personally effected by the way His members are treated: *"Inasmuch as ye have done it unto one of the least of these my brethren, ye have done it unto me"* (Matt. 25:40). When Saul of Tarsus was persecuting the church, the Lord took it very personal saying *"Saul, Saul, why do you persecute me?"* (Acts 9:4). Later, Paul called the church the "corporate Christ" (1 Cor. 12:12). And when the church was splitting, he saw Christ divided (1 Cor. 1:11-13). Indeed, the church is the literal Body of Jesus Christ.

Since the church experiences oneness with Christ, when the church grows in both spiritual life and number, Jesus Christ increases . . . His Body grows larger. The Father's desire is that this expansion continue until finally, His Son fills all in all (1 Cor. 15:28; Eph. 1:23).

Properly conceived, the church is the corporate expression of the Lord Jesus. It is a shared-life community made up of once-fallen-now-redeemed people who possess Christ's indwelling life and express that life together. It is for this reason—and this reason alone—that the subject of church planting is so vital. It is because church planting is bound up with God's ultimate intention of increasing and expressing His Son on earth.

The Kingdom of God

In God's view, the church is not only the increase of His Son on earth, it is also the visible outpost of His kingdom. Put another way, the church is God's colony on earth representing His interests and His sovereign rule.

To be sure, the church is the Body of Christ, carrying out the will of the Head and offering its life for the world. The church is also the Bride of Christ, betrothed to Him until that final union at the end of the ages where God and man enter marital oneness. Nevertheless, the church is also the community of the King, displaying to men and angels Christ's Lordship in the earth. As Stuart Murray says,

If they are functioning properly, churches will be agents of the kingdom, signposts of the kingdom, sacraments of the kingdom, provisional representations of the kingdom, proclaiming and demonstrating the kingdom, pointing to what is coming when the kingdom is fully established . . . (Church Planting: Laying Foundations)

Along the same line, Melvin Hodges writes,

The true church is the present manifestation of the kingdom of God . . . The church is God's agent in the earth—the medium through which He expresses Himself to the world. God has no other redeeming agency in the earth. (A Guide to Church Planting)

The kingdom of God is more than the invisible realm in which God lives. It is the sphere where God rules and where His rule is observed. Therefore, when a people are submitting to His rule in their lives, the kingdom is present. As R. Paul Stevens says,

The kingdom is the rule of the sovereign (God expressing His will and powerful presence) plus the response of the subjects (as they yield to the sway of the sovereign). Rule without response is less than the kingdom. In this matter the Queen of England provides a graphic model of how many Christians inadvertently regard the King. Queen Elizabeth reigns but she does not rule. And many so-called Christians defer to the position of God as supreme ruler, but in actuality do not respond as subjects. The kingdom involves both rule and response. (The Abolition of the Laity)

The Lord Jesus embodies the kingdom of God. When in the midst of the Pharisees, they asked Him when the kingdom of God will come. His answer: *"The kingdom of God comes not with observation: Neither shall they say, Here! or, there! for, behold, the kingdom of God is in the midst of you" (Luke 17:20-21).* The Lord was telling the Pharisees that He—Jesus Himself—*is* the kingdom of God, for He was in their midst at that moment.[1] In the words of Howard Snyder,

---

[1] Some have mistakenly interpreted Jesus' words here to be "the kingdom of God is within you"—which would mean that the kingdom was "inside" the Pharisees! Eminent NT scholar George E. Ladd writes, "The phrase *entos hymon* can mean either 'within you', i.e. in your hearts, or 'in your midst.' While Mark 10:15 makes it clear that the kingdom is to be received in the inner person, it is unlikely that Jesus would have said to the Pharisees, 'the kingdom of God is within *you.* ' The translation 'in your midst,' in Jesus' person, best fits the total context of His teaching." *A Theology of the New Testament* (Grand Rapids: Eerdmans, 1993), p. 65.

The gospel intends to call persons to the Body of Christ, that is, the community of believers with Jesus Christ as its essential and sovereign Head. So the church is God's agent for establishing His kingdom. It is the primary means by which He is accomplishing His reconciling purpose. Therefore, the church is inseparable from God's cosmic design to sum up all things in Jesus Christ (Eph. 1:10)—the essence and goal of the kingdom . . . The kingdom actually appeared in space and time in the very person of Jesus . . . What then is the kingdom of God? It is Jesus Christ and, through the church, the uniting of all things in Him . . . The Scriptures emphasize the eternal purpose or plan or will of God, that which He is doing in history to bring about the reconciliation of all things. This Divine purpose is identified with the kingdom or reign of God. (The Community of the King)

The Kingdom and the Church

Jesus Christ is the incarnation of joy, peace, and righteousness. When God's people are living under His rule (the kingdom), they experience His joy, His peace and His righteousness. Such is the experience of the church according to Paul:

> *For the kingdom of God is not a matter of eating and drinking, but of righteousness, peace and joy in the Holy Spirit. (Rom. 14:17)*

The purpose of the church is to make visible the kingdom, which is "now" but "not yet." At this moment Jesus Christ is reigning in spirit (the kingdom is "now"). But at a future date, He will physically reign over all the earth (the kingdom is "not yet").

As Christians, we live in the overlap of the kingdom. We are those for whom the end of the ages have met (1 Cor. 10:11). The powers of the new age have interrupted the old.

So we may taste the powers of the coming kingdom age today (Heb. 6:5). God's will is done in the heavenly realm. By the kingdom, He brings that will into the earth.

The kingdom of God is no small thing. It was the dominating thought of our Lord while He was on earth. Jesus spoke on it over 100 times in the Gospels. It was the subject of His first message (Mark 1:15) as well as His last (Acts 1:6). We are told He went about "preaching the kingdom of God" (Mt. 4:23; 9:35; Luke 4:43; 8:1). Later, He sent His disciples to do the same (Matt. 10:7; Luke 9:2; 10:9). Interestingly, the kingdom was the only thing that our Lord called the "Gospel"—good news. Even the book of Acts, which is a record of the church, begins and ends with the kingdom of God (Acts 1:1-3; 28:23, 31).

The church is a people who live under God's rule. That being so, the mission of the church is to extend God's liberating reign on the earth. This is because the church is the custodian of the kingdom, owning its keys for binding and loosing (Matt. 16:19). Put another way, the church is called to make the Headship of Christ a visible reality. Strikingly, Jesus Christ will not be Head over all creation until His Headship is first secured in His church (Col. 1:18). As David Shenk and Ervin Stutzman remark,

The kingdom of God becomes visible in any community whenever a cluster of people gather in Jesus' name . . . God's intention is that every congregation of believers in Jesus be a surprising revelation of the presence of the kingdom on earth. These surprising colonies of heaven are audiovisual expressions of the continuing life and ministry of Jesus in His fullness in an evil world. (Creating Communities of the Kingdom)

In the same vein, Stuart Murray explains,

> *The theme of the kingdom of God which permeated His [Jesus'] teaching, and the wholistic nature of His ministry, require church planting strategies to be set firmly within this broader understanding of mission. Jesus later told His hesitant followers: "As the Father sent me, I am sending you." Their mission was defined by this. Church planting, or any other aspect of the mission of the church, cannot be pursued in isolation but must be related to the mission of Jesus. (Church Planting: Laying Foundations)*

Significantly, Paul emphasized the kingdom in his preaching:

> *. . . Strengthening the disciples and encouraging them to remain true to the faith. "We must go through many hardships to enter the kingdom of God," they [Paul and Barnabas] said. (Acts 14:22)*

> *Paul entered the synagogue and spoke boldly there for three months, arguing persuasively about the kingdom of God. (Acts 19:8)*

> *Now I know that none of you among whom I have gone about preaching the kingdom will ever see me again. (Acts 20:25)*

> *From morning till evening he explained and declared to them the kingdom of God and tried to convince them about Jesus from the Law of Moses and from the Prophets. (Acts 28:23)*

> *Boldly and without hindrance he preached the kingdom of God and taught about the Lord Jesus Christ. (Acts 28:31)*

Paradoxically, Paul's gospel was centered on the kingdom (God's rule) as well as freedom and liberty. Paul's gospel was one of radical freedom and extreme liberty; yet it was one that held fast to the Lord's rights over His own (Gal. 5:1, 13; 1

Cor. 9:20-21; 2 Cor. 3:17; Rom. 6:13-23; 14:8). Modern Christians often hold these two themes in tension, as if they were contradictory. But the truth is that in the church of Jesus Christ, God's rule is secured in total and absolute freedom!

In Christ, there is no tension between the gospel of the kingdom and the gospel of grace—there is no disharmony between experiencing God's rulership and enjoying the freedom of the Spirit. Reconciling the paradox between Divine rulership and Christian liberty, F.F. Bruce writes,

> *Luther caught the spirit of Paul's argument excellently in his introductory sentences to "The Liberty of a Christian Man." "A Christian man is the most free lord of all, subject to none. A Christian man is the most dutiful servant of all, subject to all." "Subject to none" in respect to his liberty; "subject to all" in respect of his charity. And this is true of a Christian man because it was primarily true of Christ. ("The Grace of God and the Law of Christ" in God and The Good)*

The goal of planting churches, therefore, is to bring the kingdom of God into a city. It is to bring men and women into an encounter with the spiritual realm where Christ's rule is observed. First-century church planters showed God's people what it means to be "in Christ" as well as the meaning of "Christ in you." They presented to the saints their freedom in Christ as well as His Lordship and Headship. In so doing, Christ was magnified, God's enemy was shamed, and the physical arrival of the kingdom was hastened.

Again, God's ultimate aim is to extend His Son's beauty and reign on the earth. This aim is accomplished by planting churches in the manner that God ordained. As Shenk and Stutzman write,

> *Church planting is thus the most urgent business of human kind. It is through the creation (or planting) of churches that*

God's kingdom is extended into communities which have not yet been touched by the precious surprise of the presence of the kingdom of God in their midst. (Creating Communities of the Kingdom)

Origin Determines Destiny

In spiritual things, origin determines destiny. Therefore, the origin of a church will determine its destiny as well as its quality. Put another way, *how* a church is planted will determine its character, its effectiveness, and its future. Consider Paul's words:

I planted the seed, Apollos watered it, but God made it grow. So neither he who plants nor he who waters is anything, but only God, who makes things grow. The man who plants and the man who waters have one purpose, and each will be rewarded according to his own labor. For we are God's fellow workers; you are God's field, God's building. By the grace God has given me, I laid a foundation as an expert builder, and someone else is building on it. But each one should be careful how he builds. For no one can lay any foundation other than the one already laid, which is Jesus Christ. (1 Cor. 3:6-11)

In this passage, Paul mixes his metaphors. He speaks of the church as a field, then as a building. Church planters, therefore, are both farmers and builders. Paul compares the Corinthian church to a field in which he planted the seed. (This is where the term "church planting" is derived.) The seed is the glorious gospel of Jesus Christ that produces the church. On the term "church planter," Charles Brock writes,

The term "church planter" is rather new to many people. A church planter is a person, national or foreigner, who sows

the gospel seed in a way that a New Testament church comes to life and grows. (The Principles and Practice of Indigenous Church Planting)

But the church is also a building. Paul, the expert builder, laid the foundation. Poor workmanship and the use of cheap materials produces a defective building. In the natural, planting (farming) and building require special skills and training in those skills. So it is with those who found the church of Jesus Christ.

Origin determines destiny. Thus *what* the building is made of is of crucial importance:

If any man builds on this foundation using gold, silver, costly stones, wood, hay or straw, his work will be shown for what it is, because the Day will bring it to light. It will be revealed with fire, and the fire will test the quality of each man's work. (1 Cor. 3:12-13)

Jesus Christ is the Master Builder as well as the Building Inspector. He will test every work to try its integrity. While Paul's concern is with the *materials* used to build, He is also concerned with *how* the house is built. He writes,

But let each one take heed HOW he builds . . . (1 Cor. 3:10)

So in 1 Corinthians 3, we are presented with three central ingredients for planting healthy churches: 1) The competence of the church builder, 2) The materials that are used for the building, and 3) The way the house is built. In the following pages, we will focus on each ingredient as it relates to church planting in the first century.

Then I said to them, "You see the trouble we are in: Jerusalem lies in ruins, and its gates have been burned with fire. Come, let us rebuild the wall of Jerusalem, and we will no longer be in disgrace."
-Nehemiah, the prophet

SECTION 1:

FIRST-CENTURY PRINCIPLES OF CHURCH PLANTING

This section examines the ways in which churches were planted in the first century. It also treats the way church planters were prepared for their ministry. By today's standards these ways are novel; yet in reality they are ancient, long forgotten, and in need of recovery. The following pages do not contain a plea to crassly or woodenly replicate the details of NT church practice. Instead, they contain a plea to re-examine some of the basic underlying principles of how a church is born.

It is the depravity of institutions and movements that given in the beginning to express life, they often end in throttling that very life. Therefore, they need constant review, perpetual criticism and continuous bringing back to the original purposes and spirit. The Christian church is no exception. It is the chief illustration of the above.
        -E. Stanley Jones

CHAPTER 1

THE DIVINE PATTERN OF CHURCH PLANTING

Over the last 50 years, there have been nearly 100 books written on the subject of church planting. Some of these books seem to have the subject nailed down to a fine science. But what is shocking is that virtually none of these books discuss the way that churches were planted in the first century. Instead, they promote the thought of man in place of God's idea of planting *His* church.

It is a profound mistake to ignore what we find in the book of Acts concerning God's way of planting churches. As Watchman Nee says,

Never let us regard these early chapters of Acts as in-applicable today. Like the book of Genesis, the Acts of the Apostles reveals the beginnings of God's ways, and what He did then sets a pattern for His work always. (Church Affairs)

The NT reveals that there are four ways that churches were planted in Century One. These ways originated with God Himself. As pragmatic as some contemporary church planting methods are, none of them can eclipse God's way of raising up an expression of His Son's Body. Each of these four ways originated in a particular city. Hence we will label them after the city where they first appeared.

The Jerusalem Model

The first way churches were planted in the first century occurred in the city of Jerusalem. Twelve apostles planted one church by the preaching of Jesus Christ (Acts 2:14-8:3). Then, after a period of time, the church multiplied by "transplantation" or "migration."[1]

Because this method began first in Jerusalem, we will call it the *Jerusalem Model.* According to the NT narrative, after an eight year period, the seeds of the Jerusalem assembly were scattered and transplanted all throughout Palestine.[2] Because of persecution, the believers in Jerusalem relocated to other locales, shared their faith, and churches sprang up as a result (Acts 8:1-8; 11:19-21). The twelve apostles remained in the city.[3]

One of the most outstanding characteristics of the Jerusalem dispersion is that all of the saints had experienced church life *before* they relocated to form new churches. That is, they brought to other regions their *experience* of Christ and the church. This is a vital point as we will later see.

Significantly, the newly transplanted churches that scattered throughout Palestine received the help of extra-local workers—even though they were not directly planted by them. The twelve apostles circulated to each of them so as to water the seeds and pull up any emerging weeds (Acts 9:32-11:30). While the apostles helped these churches, they did not live in them nor did they control their affairs. The Twelve

---

[1] Note that the images of *planting* and *transplantation* are that of organic farming. This is because the church is an organic, biotic life—1 Cor. 3:6-8; 9:1-7.

[2] All chronological dating used in this book is based upon the *Berkeley Version* of the Bible.

[3] Keep in mind that while the twelve apostles did not leave the city of Jerusalem for eight years, the church in Jerusalem was extremely large. It numbered in the thousands. Consequently, the situation called for over ten "sent ones" to establish the ground floor of that church. All of these factors make Jerusalem, the first church on earth, unique.

itinerantly visited and strengthened the freshly budding churches in Judea, Galilee, and Samaria.

The Antioch Model

The principal way in which churches were birthed in the first century began in Antioch of Syria. It is most clearly observed in Acts 13:1-20:38. In these chapters, we learn that Paul and his co-workers were sent out from Antioch, Syria to establish churches in South Galatia, Greece, and Asia Minor. Thus this way of planting churches can be called the *Antioch Model*. It can also be called "fresh seed planting."[4]

(Incidentally, Paul's journeys are best described as "church planting trips" or "apostolic journeys." The popular term "missionary journey" was created in the 19th century and is a poor fit with the nature and goal of Paul's trips.)[5]

---

[4] C. Peter Wagner and John Wimber have called this method "catalytic church planting." Gene Edwards calls it "the Antioch line."

[5] The term "missionary journey" finds its origin in 19th century German commentaries on Paul. It was probably influenced by the fact that the 18th and 19th centuries saw the rise of world missionary work coupled with economic exploitation of India, Africa, the Orient and elsewhere by Europeans. (The commentaries of A. Schlatter confirm this.) As far as I know, the earliest reference to "missionary journey" in English is in David Thomas' *A Homiletic Commentary on the Acts of the Apostles* published in 1870. The word "mission" was not used to refer to human outreach until the 16th century. Before that time, it was used to refer to the sending of Jesus by the Father and the sending of the Spirit by the Father and Son (John 17:18). The Jesuits were the first to use the term "mission" to refer to the spreading of the Christian faith. In time, the word "mission" came to be used to refer to the sending of people across frontiers to propagate the Christian faith, convert the heathen, plant churches, and improve society (R. Paul Stevens, *The Abolition of the Laity,* Carlisle: Paternoster Press, 1999, p. 192).

The *Antioch Model* can be described thusly: A Christian worker was sent to a town to preach Jesus Christ.[6] He did not preach the "Four Spiritual Laws," the "Roman road," the "plan of salvation," or Christian theology. Nor did he preach himself (2 Cor. 4:5). Instead, he preached a Person—*Jesus Christ.*[7] Along this line, Watchman Nee writes,

> *Spiritual ministry is nothing less that ministering Christ to His people. God's thought in giving these men as a gift to His church was that a Christ, personally known and experienced by them, might through the gifts of the Spirit, be ministered to His people. (The Normal Christian Church Life)*

Speaking in the same vein, Roland Allen remarks,

> *In the Bible the preaching of Christ is not so purely intellectual, the apprehension of Christian doctrine is not so purely intellectual. What Christ asks of His disciples is not so much exposition of doctrine about Him as witness to His power . . . To make converts to a doctrine is to make proselytes. The proselyte abandons one system of thought and practice for another; and to adopt a new system of thought and practice is not the way of salvation. The Christian convert is a convert not to a system of doctrine but to Christ. (The Spontaneous Expression of the Church)*

Michael Grant says the following about the early apostles:

> *They preached a person. Their message was frankly Christocentric. Indeed, the gospel is referred to simply as Jesus or Christ: "He preached Jesus to him . . ." Jesus the man, Jesus*

---

[6] The NT uses the term "worker" to refer to those who plant churches. In the first-century, workers often traveled in pairs, but not always.
[7] See Acts 2:22-36; 8:5,12,35; 9:17-20; 10:38-43; 11:19-20;17:2-3; Rom. 16:25; Gal. 3:1; 1 Cor. 2:2; 2 Cor. 4:5.

crucified, Jesus risen, Jesus exalted to the place of power in the universe . . . Jesus who meantime was present among His people in the Spirit . . . The risen Christ was unambiguously central in their message. (Evangelism in the Early Church)

Melvin Hodges adds,

The apostolic message was completely Christ-centered . . . The message that plants churches today must likewise be Christ-centered . . . The church is brought into existence by the preaching of the gospel. We have a message that plants churches. (A Guide to Church Planting)

New converts were made as a result of the preaching of Jesus Christ. Some of them were religious people who had a relationship with God already.[8] Others had never met God.[9]

After leading people into a real encounter with Christ, the worker showed the young church how to live by the indwelling life of its newly found Lord. He disclosed to them the eternal purpose of God, which became their consuming vision. In short, the worker imparted into the spirits of the believing community the same "heavenly vision" that he himself had received.

The worker also passed on to the new church the apostolic tradition that originated with Jesus (1 Cor. 11:2; 2 Thess. 2:15; 3:6). This includes teaching and reminding the saints about the words of Jesus as well as His acts on earth.

The worker unfolded the unsearchable riches of Jesus Christ (Eph. 3:8). He unveiled to the hearts of the saints the greatness and all-sufficiency of their Lord. This is what it means to build a church on Jesus Christ as the foundation

---

[8] In the first-century, it was the religious Jews.
[9] The heathen, Gentiles.

(Matt. 7:24ff.; Matt. 16:16-18; 1 Cor. 3:11; Eph. 2:20). Having Christ as foundation means that the church learns to wholly depend upon and rest on Him for all things.

The aftermath of such ministry is that the newly founded church stood awash with the glories of Jesus Christ. First-century workers themselves had a glorious, breath-taking revelation of Christ pouring out of their own spirits before they could impart it to others. Note Paul's words:

> *God was pleased to REVEAL HIS SON IN ME, IN ORDER THAT I MIGHT PREACH HIM . . . (Gal. 1:15-16)*

The immediate and long-lasting fruit of this heavenly disclosure was this: God's people fell in love with their Lord and with one another. And they were grounded upon nothing but Christ.

In effect, the worker instructed the believers how to live by the Christ who indwelt them. He showed them how to fellowship with Him together and individually. He equipped them to function corporately under the Lord's direct Headship without any human officiation. The worker also prepared the saints for some of the trials that they would someday face (Acts 14:22; 20:31; 1 Thess. 3:4). The worker's ministry was not only spiritual, but intensely practical.[10] Speaking of Paul's message, Roland Allen observes:

> *He administered a gospel, not a law . . . This is the most distinctive mark of Pauline Christianity. He did what separates his doctrine from all other systems of religion. He did not come merely to teach a higher truth, or a finer morality*

---

[10] Most of Paul's letters follow a similar pattern: First he deals with spiritual reality (e.g., Eph. 1-3; Rom. 1-11), then he deals with practical matters (e.g., Eph. 4-6; Rom. 12-16).

*than those who preceded him. He came to administer a spirit
. . . They needed life. Christ came to give men that life, and St.
Paul came as the minister of Christ, to lead men to Christ
who is the life, that in Him they might find life. His gospel
was a gospel of power . . . He gave place for Christ. He was
always glad when his converts could progress without his aid.
He welcomed their liberty . . . He gave freely, and then he
retired from them that they might learn to exercise the powers
which they possessed in Christ. He warned them of dangers,
but did not provide an elaborate machinery to prevent them
from succumbing to dangers . . . to do this required great
faith . . . He believed in the Holy Ghost not merely vaguely as
a spiritual Power, but as a Person indwelling his converts. He
believed therefore in his converts. He could trust them . . . He
believed that Christ was able and willing to keep that which
he had committed to Him. (Missionary Methods: St. Paul's or
Ours?)*

After saturating the saints with Christ, the worker did the
unthinkable. He fully abandoned the church into the Lord's
hands! He gently pushed the saints out of their nest and left
them on their own. And he did so without hiring a pastor, a
clergyman, or even elders to oversee them. What is more, he
left the church on its own in its infancy and in the face of
imminent persecution!

According to the *Antioch Model*, the worker typically spent
anywhere from four to eighteen months laying the ground
floor of a church before leaving it. This means that Paul and
his co-workers would abandon a church when it was just
beginning to crawl! Elders who emerged within the assembly
were affirmed *later*, but theirs was never the task of gov-
erning the saints.

Notwithstanding, once leaving, the worker did not return to
the church for a long period of time. Anywhere from six
months to two years. This is the pattern of church planting as

shown to us by Paul after he was sent out from Antioch. What a mighty, fire-proof gospel Paul must have delivered to these new converts. What confidence in the Risen Christ he must have had to do such a startling thing as to leave a church on its own while it was still in diapers. Roland Allen astutely observes:

> *The facts are these: St. Paul preached in a place for five or six months and then left behind him a church, not indeed free from the need of guidance, but capable of growth and expansion . . . The question before us is, how he could so train his converts as to be able to leave them after so short a time with any security that they would be able to stand and grow. It seems at first sight almost incredible . . . What could he have taught them in five or six months? (Missionary Methods: St. Paul's or Ours?)*

Dan Cole adds,

> *On his first two journeys, Paul and his traveling companions—first Barnabas and then Silas—set fairly rigorous itineraries. They headed for the capital cities of districts and provinces, preached in local synagogues, gathered those who responded—both Jews and Gentiles—into new church units, and then moved on. Their purpose was to remain only long enough to help a new church get established. ("Into the Heart of Paganism," Christian History, Issue 47, p. 20)*

The net effect of such an alarming move is that the worker's gospel was tested to its core. If the gospel he delivered was indeed Christ, or as Paul put it—if it was comprised of "gold, silver, and precious stone"—the church would stand through the crises that it would pass through (1 Cor. 3:6-15). The brothers and sisters would continue to follow the Lord *together* when the fire fell on them. (The *church* will always face a crisis to test its foundations.) On the other hand, if the gospel that the worker brought was "wood, hay, and stubble," it would burn to the ground as soon as the heat came to try it.

Further, if a worker planted the church properly, all it needed to survive would spontaneously develop within it. In time, prophets, shepherds, evangelists, overseers, etc. would naturally emerge—just as naturally as the physical members develop on an infant as it matures.

Such development is basic to all life forms. A rose seed has within its germ a stem, leaves, and a budding flower. If the seed is planted and properly nurtured, these features will naturally manifest themselves in time. In the same way, the requisite gifts and ministries of the church naturally develop within her when it is planted and nurtured properly—for they are built into her very DNA.

Because the church is an organism and not an organization, it develops naturally when the agent who planted it leaves it on its own. But he must return periodically to water it, fertilize it, and pull up the weeds that seek to choke its life. Hence, a large part of a worker's task is to keep foreign elements out of the church so that it can grow naturally.

This understanding of church development is in stark contrast to the prevalent method of trying to appoint various ministries and gifts (like elders, prophets, and teachers) on the basis of a *pro forma* adherence to a "NT church pattern." Such a mechanical method of church formation will only produce a pathetic, paper-thin image of the church. The approach is like trying to create a mature rose by locating stem, leaves and petals, then stringing them together with nylon thread.

By contrast, the *Antioch Model* rests wholly on the presupposition that the church is born by the presentation of Jesus Christ. And that it organically grows in the absence of the founding worker after he leaves it on its own. Yet it requires his return to oversee the church's growth and keep foreign elements from choking and corrupting its life (Acts 13-20). As Howard Snyder says,

> *. . . church growth is a matter of removing the hindrances to growth. The church will naturally grow if not limited by unbiblical barriers. (The Community of the King)*

The *Antioch Model*, or "fresh seed planting," is the classic way the church was raised up in the first century. Again, Roland Allen astutely observes,

> *In a very few years, he [Paul] built the church on so firm a basis that it could live and grow in faith and in practice, that it could work out its own problems, and overcome all dangers and hindrances both from within and without. (Missionary Methods: St. Paul's or Ours?)*

In the *Jerusalem Model*, the church leaves the worker. In the *Antioch Model*, the worker leaves the church. But the end product is the same: Once the foundation of a church is laid by a worker, God's people are left on their own without his on-site help. Comparing the *Antioch* and *Jerusalem Models*, Watchman Nee writes,

> *We find there are two ways of preaching the gospel and of establishing churches—two distinct methods illustrated respectively by Jerusalem and Antioch. From Antioch apostles go forth; from Jerusalem scattered saints go forth. In the one case, bands of apostles move out—it may be Paul and Barnabas, or Paul and Silas, or Paul and Timothy—to preach the gospel from place to place, to form churches, and to return. In the other case, those who believe emigrate to new cities and new lands, preaching and telling of the Lord Jesus wherever they go; and wherever these who migrate are found, churches spring up . . . Hence we have discovered three things: that the work is regional, that it operates from*

Divinely chosen centers, and that the movement is two-fold, by workers who go and return, and by the migration of scattered saints. (Church Affairs)

The Ephesian Model

A third method of church planting is only seen once in the NT. It began in the city of Ephesus. Thus it can be called the *Ephesian Model.* In his later years, Paul traveled to Ephesus. Before he came to Ephesus, he had planted approximately eight churches over a period of seven years.

What Paul accomplished in Ephesus was as unique as it was brilliant. He made Ephesus a training center from which the gospel would go forth and where men would be equipped to plant new churches. Paul rented a meeting place called "the Hall of Tyrannus" where he preached and taught every day from 11 a.m. to 4 p.m.[11] This part of the training went on for two solid years. The men who Paul trained in Ephesus were:

- Titus from Antioch, Syria.
- Timothy from Lystra.
- Gaius from Derbe.
- Aristarchus from Thessalonica.
- Secundus from Thessalonica.
- Sopator from Berea.
- Tychicus from Ephesus.
- Trophimus from Ephesus.

---

[11] The Western Text of Acts 19:9 says that Paul used the hall from "the fifth hour to the tenth" (from 11 a.m. to 4 p.m.). F.F. Bruce points out that this reading is quite probable. See F.F. Bruce, *The Book of the Acts (Revised): The New International Commentary on the New Testament* (Grand Rapids: Eerdmans, 1988), p. 366; F.F. Bruce, *Paul: Apostle of the Heart Set Free* (Grand Rapids: Eerdmans, 1977), p. 290.

We can also add Epaphras to this list, for it appears that Paul led him to the Lord while he was in Ephesus.[12] Sometime afterwards, Epaphras, who was from Colossae, planted three churches in the Lycus valley of Asia Minor in the cities of Colossae, Laodicea, and Hierapolis (Col. 1:7; 4:12-13). As NT scholar Donald Guthrie says,

> *It must have been during this period, for instance, that the churches at Colossae, Laodicea, and Hierapolis, all in the Lycus valley, were established, although Paul himself did not visit them. Men like Epaphras and Philemon, who were known to the apostle, possibly came under his influence in the hall of Tyrannus. (The Apostles)*

In the same vein, F.F. Bruce writes,

> *To this great city, then, Paul came . . . and stayed there for the best part of three years, directing the evangelization of Ephesus itself and of the province as a whole. Plainly he was assisted in this work by a number of colleagues—like Epaphras, who evangelized the Phyrgian cities of the Lycus valley (Colossae, Laodicea, and Hierapolis)—and so effectively did they work that, as Luke puts it, "all the residents of Asia*

---

[12] Epaphras seems to be the same person known as Epaphroditus. See John L. McKenzie, S.J., *Dictionary of the Bible* (Macmillan Publishing Co., Inc.: New York, 1965), p. 239; *Matthew Henry's Commentary on the Whole Bible: Introduction to the Epistle to the Colossians.* Both Epaphroditus (Php. 2:25; 4:18) and Epaphras (Phm. 23; Col. 1:7; 4:12) were co-workers with Paul and both were with Paul during the same Roman imprisonment. Epaphras planted churches, and Paul calls Epaphroditus an *apostolos* (Php. 2:25). This all suggests that they were one person. Further, "the name occurs very frequently in inscriptions both Greek and Latin, whether at full length Epaphroditus, or in its contracted form Epaphras" (Lightfoot, *Philippians, 123*).

heard the word of the Lord's, both Jews and Greeks." (Paul: Apostle of the Heart Set Free)

While the NT does not explicitly say that Paul trained eight men in Ephesus, it strongly implies it. Consider the following points:

- All of these men were present in Ephesus with Paul during his lengthy season there.[13] Just as the Twelve lived with Jesus for three and a half years, so these eight men lived with Paul for approximately the same amount of time.

- Each of these eight men served as representatives from their churches to bring a financial contribution to Jerusalem. However, instead of traveling directly to Jerusalem with their contribution, they met Paul in Ephesus with their contributions and remained there with him for three years. Timothy and Gaius were from Galatia, which is much closer to Jerusalem than Ephesus. Therefore, there must have been a special purpose for them to accompany Paul in Ephesus for that period of time: It was so they might be trained by him.

---

[13] The following passages of Scripture put all eight men in Ephesus during the time that Paul was there: Acts 19:22; 20:4; 21:29; 1 Cor. 4:17; 16:10, 20 (Paul wrote 1 Corinthians from Ephesus). One can infer that Titus is there since Luke never mentions him throughout Acts, yet we know he is present on many occasions from Paul's letters. We learn from 2 Corinthians 8 that Titus represented Corinth for the Jerusalem relief fund, and it is clear from the letter to Titus that Paul trained him.

- Paul spoke at the Hall of Tyrannus for five hours a day for two years. The intensity of his ministry has all the marks of training on it.

- Paul paid for his own needs and the needs of these men (Acts 20:34). Why would he support them if he was not training them?

- After the Ephesian trip, Paul sent these men out to work with the churches he planted as well as to plant churches in new territories.[14] This is similar to Jesus sending out the Twelve on their trial mission (Mark 6:7).

David Shenk and Ervin Stutzman sum up the *Ephesian Model* nicely:

. . . Paul sometimes stayed in one location for a couple of weeks or months, and then pressed on to begin a new ministry. That is only part of the story. He also put his roots into communities where it was necessary for the church to be firmly established. One such community was Ephesus. Paul invested three full years in that city . . . When Paul left Ephesus, he took with him a cluster of persons to visit some of the churches which he had planted in Macedonia and Greece. We may assume these persons were leaders he had trained in Ephesus. He wanted them to see the churches he told them about in his church planting classes. These persons included Sopater, Aristarchus, Secundus, Gaius, Timothy, Tychicus, and Trophimus. He wanted these leaders experienced in church development in Asia also to experience Christian fellowship in European churches. This journey was a cross-cultural church planting trip for the leaders whom

---

[14] See p. 49.

Paul was training . . . Paul kept in constant contact with the persons he had trained for ministry. He wrote two letters to Timothy . . . He wrote in the same manner to Titus . . . These letters explicitly demonstrate that Paul stayed in contact with those he trained for ministry. (Creating Communities of the Kingdom)

During the Ephesian training, Paul sent the eight men all over Asia Minor to preach the gospel of Christ and plant new churches. Some of these churches are listed in Revelation 2 and 3. F.F. Bruce writes,

While Paul stayed in Ephesus, a number of his colleagues carried out missionary activity in neighboring cities. During those years his colleague Epaphras appears to have evangelized the cities of the Lycus valley, Colossae, Laodicea, and Hierapolis—cities which Paul evidently did not visit in person (Col. 1:7-8; 2:1; 4:12-13). Perhaps all seven of the churches in Asia addressed in the Revelation of John were also founded about this time. The province was intensely evangelized, and remained one of the leading centers of Christianity for many centuries. (The Book of the Acts)

Donald Guthrie confirms the point saying,

. . . Since there were seven churches in Asia (excluding Colossae and Hierapolis) when the apocalypse of John was written, it is highly probable that these were founded during the period of Paul's Ephesian ministry. (The Apostles)

The Roman Model

The fourth and final way that churches were planted in the first century is illustrated by the church in Rome. It can be called "inverted transplantation." In the *Jerusalem Model,* one church transplants itself into many different cities, thus creating many different churches. But in the *Roman Model,* Christians living in many different churches transplant themselves into one city to found one new church. This is what appears to have happened in Rome, Italy.

The evidence for this is powerful. Not a few NT scholars have argued that Romans 16 was not written to the church in Rome, but to the church in Ephesus. The reason? Because Paul knew all of the people listed in that chapter, some of whom had lived in Ephesus. Paul had never been to Rome. Others have argued that the people Paul greets in Romans 16 coincidentally moved to Rome and all ended up in the same church. These two theories are implausible as we shall shortly see.

It seems that the original Roman church was primarily Jewish. Luke tells us that visitors from Rome came to Jerusalem on the day of Pentecost and heard Peter preach the gospel (Acts 2:10). It appears that some of them returned to Rome and began to gather there. Priscilla and Aquila were probably part of this group. However, in A.D. 49, Emperor Claudius passed an edict which had all the Jews expelled from Rome.

When Paul writes his letter to the Romans in A.D. 57, Jews are back in the church. Many Gentiles are there now also. Paul greets 26 individuals and five households, all of whom he knows personally. Virtually all of them have come from the various churches he planted over the years.

The scenario that best fits the evidence is that Paul sent Priscilla and Aquila back to Rome once Claudius' edict was lifted in A.D. 54. One clue that supports this view is how Priscilla and Aquila helped Paul plant the church in Ephesus. Four years before Paul wrote his famous Roman letter, he brought this remarkable couple to Ephesus and left them there to labor before he returned to plant the Ephesian church (Acts

18:18-19). NT scholars William Sanday and Arthur Headlam write,

That Prisca and Aquila should be at Rome is just what we might expect from one with so keen an eye for the strategy of a situation as St. Paul. When he was himself established and in full work at Ephesus with the intention of visiting Rome, it would at once occur to him what valuable work they might be doing there and what an excellent preparation they might make for his own visit, while in his immediate surroundings they were almost superfluous. So that instead of presenting any difficulty, that he should send them back to Rome where they were already known, is most natural. (A Critical and Exegetical Commentary on the Epistle to the Romans)

After sending Priscilla and Aquila to Rome, Paul then asked various individuals, both Jew and Gentile, from the various churches he planted to move to Rome.[15] The goal? To plant a cosmopolitan church of Jew and Gentile in a cosmopolitan city.

This reconstruction fits the evidence much better than to assume that Romans 16 is part of the Ephesian letter and was misplaced with the letter to the Romans. There is no strong textual or manuscript evidence that would warrant that we separate Romans 16 from the Roman epistle.[16] It is also more

---

[15] He also asked some of his Jewish kinfolk from Jerusalem to relocate to Rome (Rom. 16:7).

[16] Douglas Moo successfully refutes the idea that Romans 16 is not part of the Roman letter in his *Epistle to the Romans: New International Commentary of the New Testament* (Grand Rapids: Eerdmans, 1996), pp. 5-9.

reasonable than the idea that the 26 individuals coincidentally relocated to Rome in the space of only three years.[17]

Further, in Romans 15:20, Paul makes plain that he will not build a church on another man's foundation. Yet he talks to the Romans as their apostle. And in Romans 1:15, he says that he will preach the gospel in Rome when he arrives there. Several scholars working in the field of epistolography conclude that Paul sends his greetings in order to make evident the nature of his relationship with the saints in Rome and thus establishes his apostolic authority there.[18]

Piecing all of the evidence together, therefore, we discover that Paul is the worker in Rome by inverted transplantation. This scenario explains how Paul could know all of the people he greets in Romans 16 without disconnecting it from the Roman letter. It also gives us insight into yet another way of planting the church of Jesus Christ.

The Team Concept

The NT clearly shows that God is a fan of workers laboring in teams, particularly in pairs. This is not *always* the case throughout Scripture, for Paul, Peter, Timothy, Titus, Epaphras, et al. labored in some places alone.[19] However, the general rule is that the work was accomplished by men who labored together.[20] Note the following:

---

[17] Priscilla and Aquila moved to Rome sometime after the Spring of A.D. 54, when Claudius' ban was lifted. The letter to the Romans was written in the winter of A.D. 57.

[18] See Jervis, Welma, and Gamble.

[19] Acts 9:32ff.; 1 Thess. 3:2, 5; Col. 4:12-13; Titus 3:12; 2 Tim. 4:20.

[20] This does not mean that one of the workers was not in the "lead" when they traveled together. A careful reading of the NT makes this clear. Paul, for instance, was the "chief speaker" when he and Barnabas labored together in Lystra (Acts 14:12).

- The twelve apostles are listed in pairs (Matt. 10:2-4).
- Jesus sent out the Twelve in pairs for a trial mission (Mark 6:7).
- Jesus sent out the 70 in pairs for a field assignment (Luke 10:1).
- The Twelve (minus Judas) are listed in pairs when Luke mentions them in the upper room (Acts 1:13)
- The Lord often sent a pair of His disciples to serve Him with some task (Matt. 21:1; Luke 22:8).
- Peter and John worked together as a pair (Acts 3:1ff.; 4:13ff.; 8:14ff.).
- Paul and Barnabas worked together as a pair (Acts 13-15:35).
- Barnabas and Mark worked together as a pair (Acts 15:39).
- Paul and Silas worked together as a pair (Acts 15:40).
- Paul sent pairs of men to serve in the work (Acts 19:22; 2 Cor. 8:16-18).

Centers for the Work

In the first century, workers were sent out from a particular church. They then returned to that church after a church planting trip to give a report of the work (Acts 14:27; 15:4).[21] The churches that sent the workers out served as "centers" for the work. Jerusalem was such a center. So was Antioch.

The twelve apostles were sent from Jerusalem to found and nourish churches in Palestine. Peter, for instance, left Jerusalem and labored in Samaria, Lydda, Joppa, and Caesarea.

---

[21] The Twelve did the same when Jesus sent them out on a trial mission (Mark 6:30; Luke 9:10).

But he always returned back to Jerusalem to give a report and to rest (Acts 8-11).

Antioch was a center for Paul. Paul went to Galatia, then returned to Antioch to give a report and to rest (Acts 13-14). He then left Antioch and went to Greece to labor. Afterwards he returned to Antioch again to give a report and to rest (Acts 15-18). William McBirnie remarks,

> *Antioch was his [Paul's] home base. This is where the Holy Spirit said, "Separate Paul and Barnabas unto Me and send them" . . . Paul started churches like a string of pearls all over the route of the circle which he traveled on his first journey, but the pearls led back home and clasped together at Antioch. (The Search for the Early Church)*

Watchman Nee adds,

> *So today we see how the work of God operates regionally. God would have His work in an area centered in one place, from which workers go and to which they return . . . So Peter moves to and from Jerusalem. Later, Paul moves to and from Antioch. They do not settle permanently in other places, but always return to their starting point. (Church Affairs)*

Strategy for Spontaneous Expansion

There is another point worth mentioning that has to do with Paul's church planting strategy.[22] Paul was an urban church

---

[22] The exact strategy that the apostles used in their preaching to the lost is beyond the scope of this book. However, there were two major venues for it: The principle of the marketplace (Acts 17:17), where the gospel is preached to a heathen audience and the principle of the synagogue (Acts 17:1-3), where the gospel is preached to a religious audience. While Paul's calling was primarily to the Gentile (Gal. 2:7-9), he preached to the Jew

planter. For the most part, he by-passed the rural areas and ignored the small communities.[23] Instead, he went directly to the major urban areas. He concentrated on planting churches in *influential* cities that had large populations.

It is for this reason that the word "pagan" has come to refer to non-Christian people. The word "pagan" is derived from the ancient word for "farmer," our country-dweller. (A similar etymology lies behind the word "heathen." The heathens are those who live on the "heath," that is, out in the country.)

Christianity was never successful outside the cities of the ancient world. Because Christianity is inherently relational, the church was unable to successfully take root outside urban settings. In urban areas, Christians could see one another in their day-to-day lives and easily care for one another. In the countryside, the believers were more isolated from each other and had a difficult time fleshing out all the *"one anothers"* that the NT emphasizes.[24] Hence, Christianity, historically, has been dominantly urban.

But Paul's strategy in planting churches in large cities went beyond making it conducive for community life. It was also to allow the gospel to spread spontaneously (e.g., 1 Thess. 1:8). The church, when properly functioning, will draw the lost by her sheer magnetism and charm. In the big city where there is no shortage of people who live in close proximity, this is feasible. In the country-yard, it is far more difficult.

---

first (Rom. 1:16). Inversely, while Peter's calling was primarily to the Jew (Gal. 2:7-9), he preached to the Gentile as well (Acts 10:1ff.). There was, therefore, considerable overlap between the callings of the two men. Further, both men labored in Judea, Antioch, Corinth, Rome, Galatia, and Asia.

[23] The exceptions are found in Derbe (a small town) and the "surrounding regions" around Lycaonia (Acts 14:6).

[24] See *Who is Your Covering?*, pp. 36-37.

Speaking of "the spontaneous expansion of the church," Roland Allen writes,

This then is what I mean by spontaneous expansion. I mean the expansion which follows the unexhorted and unorganized activity of individual members of the church explaining to others the gospel which they have found for themselves; I mean the expansion which follows the irresistible attraction of the Christian church for men who see its ordered life, and are drawn to it by desire to discover the secret of a life which they instinctively desire to share; I mean also the expansion of the church by the addition of new churches. (The Spontaneous Expansion of the Church)

C. Peter Wagner makes a similar point saying,

The single most effective evangelistic methodology under heaven is planting new churches . . . Church planting is the New Testament way of extending the gospel. Trace the expansion of the church through Jerusalem, Judea, Samaria, and the uttermost part of the earth and you will see that church planters led the way. This is a kingdom activity, strongly endorsed by God our King. (Church Planting for a Greater Harvest)

Pisidian Antioch, Philippi, Thessalonica, Corinth, Ephesus, Rome were not sleepy little towns. They were strategic cities where spontaneous expansion could easily occur. F.F. Bruce remarks,

So Paul traveled along the Roman highways, the main lines of communication, preaching the gospel and planting churches in strategic centres. From those centres the saving message would be disseminated . . . (Paul: Apostle of the Heart Set Free)

Strikingly, in Paul's mind, an entire province was evangelized if he planted a few churches in the central cities that belonged to it. When Paul wrote his letter to the Romans, he and his co-workers had planted less than 20 churches in Galatia, Greece, Asia Minor, and Rome. Even so, to Paul's mind, the gospel had been fully preached from Jerusalem all the way to Rome!

In only ten years with less than 20 Gentile churches on the planet, Paul felt there was no further place for him to preach in the regions from Jerusalem to Rome! (Rom. 15:19-24). Donald Guthrie makes the point saying,

Turning to his immediate plans, he [Paul] makes the astonishing statement that he finds no further room for work in the regions just mentioned. This does not mean that the areas have been completely evangelized, for Paul's strategy was to plant churches in important centers and then to expect the developing churches to evangelize the surrounding district. Only by this means was he able to work in so many areas. (The Apostles)

Roland Allen adds,

In little more than ten years St. Paul established the church in four provinces of the Empire, Galatia, Macedonia, Achaia, and Asia. Before AD 47 there were no churches in these provinces; in AD 57 St. Paul could speak as if his work there was done, and could plan extensive tours into the far west without anxiety lest the churches which he founded might perish in his absence for want of his guidance and support . . . St. Paul's theory of evangelizing a province was not to preach in every place in it himself, but to establish centres of Christian life in two or three important places from which the knowledge might spread into the country abroad . . . By establishing the church in two or three centres St. Paul claimed that he had evangelized the whole province . . . When he had occupied two or three centres he had really and effectually occupied the province. (Missionary Methods: St. Paul's or Ours?)

The Leadership of the Holy Spirit

Because workers are sent by God,[25] the work belongs to God and not to the worker. Accordingly, the Lord orchestrates and pioneers His own work. He chooses where the gospel is to be preached and where workers are to travel. He also engineers the timing that His work should be done. Consider the following passages that make this plain:

About noon the following day as they were on their journey and approaching the city, Peter went up on the roof to pray. He became hungry and wanted something to eat, and while the meal was being prepared, he fell into a trance. He saw heaven opened and something like a large sheet being let down to earth by its four corners. While Peter was still thinking about the vision, the Spirit said to him, "Simon, three men are looking for you. So get up and go downstairs. Do not hesitate to go with them, for I have sent them. (Acts 10:9-11, 19-20)

I went in response to a revelation and set before them the gospel that I preach among the Gentiles. But I did this privately to those who seemed to be leaders, for fear that I was running or had run my race in vain. (Gal. 2:2)

Paul and his companions traveled throughout the region of Phrygia and Galatia, having been kept by the Holy Spirit from preaching the word in the province of Asia. (Acts 16:6)

---

[25] The one who sends workers is God (John 20:21; Acts 13:2; 1 Cor. 1:17)! However, Divine sending today is always *through* a church, representatives of a church, or an older worker.

When they came to the border of Mysia, they tried to enter Bithynia, but the Spirit of Jesus would not allow them to. So they passed by Mysia and went down to Troas. (Acts 16:7-8)

During the night Paul had a vision of a man of Macedonia standing and begging him, "Come over to Macedonia and help us." After Paul had seen the vision, we got ready at once to leave for Macedonia, concluding that God had called us to preach the gospel to them. (Acts 16:9-10)

The following night the Lord stood near Paul and said, "Take courage! As you have testified about me in Jerusalem, so you must also testify in Rome." (Acts 23:11)

Crispus, the synagogue ruler, and his entire household believed in the Lord; and many of the Corinthians who heard him believed and were baptized. One night the Lord spoke to Paul in a vision: "Do not be afraid; keep on speaking, do not be silent. For I am with you, and no one is going to attack and harm you, because I have many people in this city." So Paul stayed for a year and a half, teaching them the word of God. (Acts 18:8-11)

Watchman Nee articulates a most important spiritual principle concerning where a worker is to labor saying,

An apostle should go and work in a certain place if the local church invites him, or if he himself has received a revelation from the Lord to work there . . . There are two lines which regulate the work of an apostle—he must either have a direct revelation of God's will, or an indirect revelation through the invitation of a church. (The Normal Christian Church Life)

First-century workers possessed spiritual discernment. They were not strangers to the Lord's inward guidance (1 Cor. 2:7-16). For after all, it is Jesus Christ who creates the church

by His Spirit. Men are but His instruments. As Charles
Chaney says,

> *Church planting is precisely the work of the Spirit . . . it is He
> who creates community; first the Holy Spirit indwells the
> gathered congregations as well as the Body of its believers .
> . . secondly, the Holy Spirit instructs the churches . . . thirdly,
> the Holy Spirit endows the churches and finally the Holy
> Spirit empowers churches. (Church Planting at the End of the
> Twentieth Century)*

Summary

To recap, the NT gives us four ways in which churches
were planted in the first century and visible communities of
the kingdom were established. They are:

- *The Jerusalem Model* — One church is transplanted
  into many different cities, thus creating many new
  churches.

- *The Antioch Model* — Workers are sent out from a
  local church to plant churches in new cities. The
  workers leave those churches on their own in their
  infancy.

- *The Ephesian Model* — An older worker resides in a
  particular city to plant a church and train younger
  workers. He then sends them out to plant new c-
  hurches in nearby regions.

- *The Roman Model* — Believers from many different
  churches transplant themselves into a specified city to
  found one new church.

These are the four means of planting churches that we find in the NT. Sadly, it is exotically rare to find anyone observing them today. Speaking to a group of Christian workers, Watchman Nee writes,

> *Though today the places we visit and the conditions we meet may be vastly different from those of the Scripture record, yet in principle the experience of the first apostles may well serve as our example . . . Christianity has lost its original purity, and everything connected with it is in a false and confused state. Despite that fact, our work today is still the same as in the days of the early apostles—to found and build up local churches, the local expressions of the Body of Christ. (The Normal Christian Church Life)*

Roland Allen echoes the same sentiment saying,

> *Today if a man ventures to suggest that there may be something in the methods by which St. Paul attained such wonderful results worthy of our careful attention, and perhaps of our imitation, he is in danger of being accused of revolutionary tendencies . . . All I can say is, "This is the way of Christ and His apostles." If any man answers, "That is out of date," or "Times have changed" . . . I can only repeat "This is the way of Christ and His apostles," and leave him to face that issue. (Missionary Methods: St. Paul's or Ours?)*

Would to God that every person who feels called to plant churches would return to first-century principles. If we will behold NT expressions of the church, we should return to the NT way of starting churches.

The person who says it cannot be done should not interrupt the person doing it.
    -Chinese Proverb

CHAPTER 2

RECOVERING THE ITINERANT WORKER

In our last chapter we examined the four ways that churches were planted in the first century. All of them are hardly known today.

In the typical institutional church, the pastor is usually the one who plants the church.[1] The pastor CEOs the church, directs all of its affairs, and performs virtually all of its ministry. The daunting results: the Headship of Christ is supplanted by human hands, Body life is hampered, and God's people never experience the meaning of Paul's words in Ephesians 4:16: "the Body builds *itself* up in love."

While most modern pastors carry on rather loudly about "equipping the saints for the work of the ministry," there is little to no fleshing out of this principle in their ministries. This is one of the reasons why pastors are the single most occupationally frustrated group in America.[2]

Most pastors would be terrified at the thought of having their work tested and their gospel put to the proof. Just let one of them leave their congregation on its own for six months without any human leadership. In so doing, the cumulative fruit of their weekly sermons would become evident.

---

[1] Most modern missionaries will install a pastor or a group of elders shortly after they start a church. So the effects are the same as what has been described above.

[2] Roughly 30% to 40% of religious leaders eventually drop out of the ministry and about 75% go through a period of stress so great that they seriously consider quitting ("Pastoral Pressure," *Clergy/Leaders* Mail List No. 850, June 25, 1999).

Such a telling move would make plain the following: Did the pastor present Christ in such a profound way that the congregation knows how to live by His indwelling life? Are the saints so equipped that they can function as a thriving organism in a coordinated, synchronized way without a human facilitator or mediator? Do they know how to minister Jesus Christ to one another without a man directing who says what?

What would happen if every modern pastor would do what Paul of Tarsus did and abandon their congregations to the absolute, functional, and practical Headship of Jesus Christ without erecting a human hierarchy over them? By this piercing litmus test (walking out on the church and entrusting it fully to the Risen Lord), the entire ministry of the modern pastor would be laid bare. The testing would quickly reveal if his ministry was made of imperishables or something less.

Interestingly, the same analysis can be applied to those men and women who have started house churches. What would happen if the person that founded the house church left it alone for six months without installing a human leader (or leaders) over it? Such a move would be most revealing.

The fact is that when a person starts a house church and remains in it, the saints naturally depend upon that person. And no matter how loudly this person screams that he is not "the pastor," the reality is that the saints will naturally look to him alone for guidance and direction. As a result, his mere presence impedes Body life and obstructs corporate leadership, irrespective of the best intentions. (Sometimes a group of men called "elders" take the position of the pastor, and they control the group in both ministry and practical affairs.)

This brings us to a critical question. What is the fundamental ingredient for planting churches NT style?

The Worker and the Work

Virtually every church in the first century was given birth at the hands of an extra-local, itinerant worker who eventually left. (Note: The few churches mentioned in the NT that emerged without the direct aid of an itinerant worker were *always* helped and encouraged by one after its birth.)

This person is known by the following names: "Apostle," "sent one," "worker," "foundation layer," "church planter," et al. The term "worker" is particularly favorable. Jesus used it in His messages (Matt. 9:37-38; 20:1-2; Luke 10:2, 7). Paul used it in his letters (1 Cor. 3:9; 2 Cor. 6:1; 11:13; Php. 3:2; Col. 4:11). And Luke referred to the ministry of planting and nurturing churches as "the work":

While they were worshiping the Lord and fasting, the Holy Spirit said, "Set apart for me Barnabas and Saul for THE WORK to which I have called them." (Acts 13:2, NIV)

From Attalia they sailed back to Antioch, where they had been committed to the grace of God for THE WORK they had now completed. (Acts 14:26)

But Paul did not think it wise to take him, because he had deserted them in Pamphylia and had not continued with them in THE WORK. (Acts 15:38)

In discussing the careful distinction between the "the work" and "the church," NT scholar Robert Banks writes,

. . . Paul's work existed as a separate entity with a life of its own alongside the local churches founded and supported by it . . . Those involved in Paul's mission were not primarily participating in a common life—though that certainly did occur—but rather sharing in a common task. Hence the

description "ergon," work, which lies at the root of so much of Paul's thinking about this. The "work" may be viewed as a sort of mobile commune in which resources were pooled . . . . Despite their different orientations, the "work" and the "churches" participate in each others' activities in various ways. Paul and those involved in other missions seek to nurture the small communities they have founded and lead them to Christian adulthood. They carry out this responsibility by making personal visits of longer or shorter duration, writing letters to help them with their problems, sending emissaries as their personal representatives, and praying constantly for their welfare and progress. But always Paul is moving on . . . The two, the church and the work, should never be confused, as they generally have been in subsequent Christian thinking. Paul views his missionary operation not as an 'ekklesia' but rather as something existing independently alongside the scattered Christian communities . . . Its [the work's] purpose is first the preaching of the gospel and the founding of churches, and then the provision of assistance so that they may reach maturity. (Paul's Idea of Community)

Watchman Nee adds,

If we are to understand the mind of God concerning His work, then we must differentiate clearly between the work and the churches. These two are quite distinct in Scripture, and we must avoid confusing them, otherwise we make serious mistakes . . . In the will of God, "the church" and "the work" follow two distinct lines. The work belongs to the apostles, whilst the churches belong to the local believers. The apostles are responsible for the work in any place, and the church is responsible for all the children of God there . . . To be an apostle means to be a sent one, i.e. to be always going out. A stationary apostle is a contradiction in terms . . . Those [first-century] believers were not like the believers of today, hoping for a settled pastor to instruct them, solve their problems and shelter them from trouble; and those apostles were not like the apostles of today; they were pioneers, not settlers. They did not wait till believers were mature before they left them. They dared to leave them in mere infancy, for they believed in the power of the life of God within them. (The Normal Christian Church Life)

Stewards of the Mystery

According to Scripture, an apostle is a "sent one." That is, he is a messenger. He is an envoy *sent* to declare—*to preach*—a message. And out of that message, a community is raised up by the Holy Spirit. Note the following passages:

And he ordained twelve, that they should be with him, and that he might SEND them forth TO PREACH. (Mark 3:14)

For Christ did not SEND me to baptize, but TO PREACH THE GOSPEL . . . (1 Cor. 1:17)

And how shall they PREACH, except they be SENT? As it is written, "How beautiful are the feet of them that PREACH THE GOSPEL OF PEACE, and bring glad tidings of good things!" (Rom. 10:15)[3]

Because first-century workers were sent, they were itinerant. They traveled. They were pioneers and explorers. But that is not all. Christian workers held in their hands a stewardship. That stewardship was to articulate the mystery of

---

[3] See also Acts 14:7, 21; 16:9-10, 20:24; Rom. 1:1, 9, 15, 16; 2:16; 15:16, 19, 20, 29; 16:25; 1 Cor. 4:15; 9:12, 16-18, 23; 15:1; 2 Cor. 2:12; 4:3, 4; 10:14, 16; 11:7; Gal. 1:11; 2:2, 5, 7, 14; 4:13; Eph. 1:13; 3:6; 6:19: Php. 1:5, 7, 12, 17, 27; Col. 1:5, 23; 1 Thess. 1:5; 2:2, 4, 8, 9; 3:2; 2 Thess. 2:14; 1 Tim. 1:11; 2 Tim. 1:8.

God to His people (1 Cor. 4:1ff.). The "mystery," as Paul called it, was the consuming revelation that burned in the hearts of all who had been sent.

One of the worker's main tasks was to impart this revelation—or vision—to the Lord's people. As Proverbs says, *"Without a vision, the people cast off restraint"* (Prov. 29:18). Without a unified vision of the Lord, God's people disintegrate—they run amuck. Without a "seeing" of Jesus Christ, they lose heart, motivation, purpose, and harmony. A shared vision of Christ has sustaining power. It also produces unity.

One of the principal tasks of the Christian worker, then, was to give language to the vision of God's mystery. First-century workers had a matchless revelation of the mystery of God's eternal purpose in Christ.[4] And they were able to articulate this mystery so that the Lord's people would apprehend it. This was a mark of Paul's ministry in planting churches. Consider the following passages:

> *Now to him that is of power to establish you according to my gospel, and the preaching of Jesus Christ, according to the revelation of the MYSTERY, which was kept secret since the world began. (Rom. 16:25)*

> *But we speak the wisdom of God in a MYSTERY, even the hidden wisdom, which God ordained before the world unto our glory . . . Now we have received, not the spirit of the world, but the spirit which is of God; that we might know the things that are freely given to us of God. Which things also we speak, not in the words which man's wisdom teacheth, but which the Holy Ghost teacheth; comparing spiritual things*

---

[4] The mystery of God is Christ, and the mystery of Christ is the church. So the "mystery" is Christ the Head and Christ the Body: One new man (Eph. 2:15; 3:4-11; 5:32; Col. 1:26-27).

with spiritual. But the natural man receiveth not the things of the Spirit of God: for they are foolishness unto him: neither can he know them, because they are spiritually discerned. (1 Cor. 2:7, 12-14)

Having made known unto us the MYSTERY of his will, according to his good pleasure which he hath purposed in himself. (Eph. 1:9)

How that by revelation he made known unto me the MYS-TERY . . . Whereby, when ye read, ye may understand my knowledge in the MYSTERY of Christ. Which in other ages was not made known unto the sons of men, as it is now revealed unto his holy apostles and prophets by the Spirit. (Eph. 3:3-5)

Unto me, who am less than the least of all saints, is this grace given, that I should preach among the Gentiles the un-searchable riches of Christ; and to make all men see what is the fellowship of the MYSTERY, which from the beginning of the world hath been hid in God, who created all things by Jesus Christ. (Eph. 3:8-9)

And for me, that utterance may be given unto me, that I may open my mouth boldly, to make known the MYSTERY of the gospel. (Eph. 6:19)

Even the MYSTERY which hath been hid from ages and from generations, but now is made manifest to his saints. (Col. 1:26)

That their hearts might be comforted, being knit together in love, and unto all riches of the full assurance of un-derstanding, to the acknowledgment of the MYSTERY of God, and of the Father, and of Christ. (Col. 2:2)

Praying also for us, that God would open unto us a door of utterance, to speak the MYSTERY of Christ, for which I am also in bonds. (Col. 4:3)

As F.F. Bruce says,

. . . the "mysteries" which he [Paul] was granted were not private experiences for his own spiritual enrichment; they were revelations of the Divine purpose and its fulfillment to be imparted for the upbuilding and healthy functioning of the whole Christian fellowship . . . His own apostolic ministry was the means in the Divine purpose for the accomplishment of this "mystery." (Paul: Apostle of the Heart Set Free)

Elsewhere Bruce writes,

. . . there was one mystery above all others—the mystery of God's loving purpose, disclosed in Christ alone—and Paul's concerns were that they [the saints] should come to know this all-surpassing mystery, and know it as an indwelling presence . . . The "mystery of Christ" into which Paul has received such exceptional insight is the content of the "revelation of Jesus Christ" of which he speaks in Gal. 1:12. Christ is Himself "the mystery of God" (Col. 2:2; cf. Col. 1:26-27) in the sense that in Him the unseen God is fully revealed; "the mystery of Christ" may best be understood as the mystery which consists in Christ, the mystery which is disclosed in Him. (The Epistles to the Colossians, to Philemon, and to the Ephesians)

A good definition of a leader is someone that knows the next step. This "knowing" is based on "seeing." Moses could not build the tabernacle without first being shown the pattern for it. In the same way, first-century workers had insight into the purpose of God. They possessed spiritual sight—the ability to see the unseen.

Paul, the model Christian worker, calls himself a "master builder" (1 Cor. 3:10). The Greek word translated "master builder" is *architekton,* from which our word "architect" is derived. This refers to the spiritual gift that gives workers the capacity to see how the different parts of the spiritual building fit with the other parts. An architect has the insight to see where the stairway fits into the living room, where the master bathroom will be located, how the plumbing must be laid out, where and when the electrical outlets must be installed, etc. It is the same with those who build God's spiritual house. As Melvin Hodges says,

The church planter will be a man of vision. He will see possibilities where others only see obstacles. He will be highly motivated and persevere in spite of discouraging setbacks. His vision is backed up by a solid faith that God has sent him to do this work and will see him through. Most churches are established because of the vision, spiritual burden, sacrifice, and perseverance of some individual who gave himself to the task of church planting. (A Guide to Church Planting)

In a word, first-century workers were those who saw the next step and had the ability to show God's people how to take it. They were gifted not only in imparting vision, but in catalyzing people to work together toward fulfilling it.

Spiritual Equippers

One of the key roles a Christian worker had in planting a church was to equip God's people to minister Christ one to another. R. Paul Stevens throws light on the phrase "to equip the saints" when he says,

The Greek word for equipping, "katartismos," is used as a noun only once—in Ephesians 4:12. But the word has an interesting medical history in classical Greek. To equip is to put a bone or a part of the human body into right relationship with the other parts of the body so that every part fits thoroughly . . . A Greek doctor would "equip" a body by putting a bone back into its correct relationship with the other members of the body. (Liberating the Laity)

How did workers equip the saints? How did they co-ordinate the various parts of the Body of Christ so that they were empowered to function? Aside from supplying the church with a revelation of the Lord, there were a number of other ingredients. The following four are most important:

(1) Removing the Sin Consciousness

One of the major obstacles that hinder God's people from functioning in an open meeting is the consciousness of sin. This is the sense of guilt. The sense of condemnation. The sense of unworthiness.

In the first century, the Christian worker's task was to empower God's people to be set free to share the Lord in a church meeting. He did so by showing them that they are blameless in God's eyes.[5] He showed them how God sees them in Christ, and that His shed blood is enough to satisfy God's demands. Helping to arm God's people with a clean conscience—where there is no consciousness of sin—empowered Christians to open their mouths boldly and share the Lord with one another (see Heb. 9:14; 10:1-25).

---

[5] Sometimes it is to teach them to repent. For if a believer is deliberately walking in sin, his conscience will be defiled. Paul's letters are dripping over with both themes: The righteousness of the saints, and at times when unrepentant sin is in the camp, the need to repent.

(2) Providing Practical Tools

Perhaps the greatest lack in today's preaching and teaching is the utter absence of practical handles regarding what is taught. Most preaching today is swimming lessons on dry land. The bulk of today's sermons are chalk-board lectures in the abstract world of ideas and theories. Either that, or they are emotional pep-talks that invoke warm fuzzies about one's self-image. In this way, modern Christianity is analogous to teaching people how to play basketball without a ball or a hoop.

Not so in the first century. The Christian worker's message was Christ. Yet as he declared the glory of God in the face of Jesus Christ, the worker had a responsibility to show God's people *how* to experience that glory by simple yet do-able means.[6]

(3) Giving People Confidence in Their Gifting

Without confidence, the people of God will stay muted and passive. Throughout Paul's letters, he reiterated again and again the confidence he had in the saints and their abilities (Gal. 5:10; 2 Thess. 3:4; 2 Cor. 2:3; 7:16; 8:22; Rom. 15:14; Php. 1:6). First-century workers showed confidence in God's work in the church and its response to God. Instilling such confidence in God's people helped empower them to function.

---

[6] Paul's letters are peppered with both the spiritual element and the practical element.

(4) Modeling by Example

As vital as the above ministry is to church formation, the *example* that the worker sets when he is among the saints is of greater importance. A church is equipped not only by preaching, but by modeling. First-century workers modeled what they preached by their own example. Paul often makes mention of this aspect:

Join with others in following my EXAMPLE, brothers, and take note of those who live according to the PATTERN we gave you. (Php. 3:17)

Because our gospel came to you not simply with words, but also with power, with the Holy Spirit and with deep conviction. You know HOW WE LIVED AMONG YOU for your sake. You became IMITATORS OF US and of the Lord; in spite of severe suffering, you welcomed the message with the joy given by the Holy Spirit. (1 Thess. 1:5-6)

For you yourselves know how you ought to follow our EXAMPLE. We were not idle when we were with you. (2 Thess. 3:7)

In everything SET THEM AN EXAMPLE BY DOING what is good. In your teaching show integrity, seriousness. (Titus 2:7)

FOLLOW MY EXAMPLE, as I follow the example of Christ. (1 Cor. 11:1)

The Non-Authoritarianism of First-Century Workers

Paul is the model Christian worker. In everything he did to care for and protect a church, he acted in the capacity of a spiritual father and mother. Consider his words:

But we were gentle among you, like a MOTHER caring for her little children. We loved you so much that we were delighted to share with you not only the gospel of God but our lives as well, because you had become so dear to us . . . For you know that we dealt with each of you as a FATHER deals with his own children, encouraging, comforting and urging you to live lives worthy of God, who calls you into his kingdom and glory. (1 Thess. 2:7-12)

. . . And I will not be burdensome to you; for I do not seek yours, but you. (2 Cor. 12:14)

Paul was a non-authoritarian. God gave him the responsibility to care for the churches he planted in multiple ways—all of which were non-authoritarian and non-coercive. As Robert Banks says,

Paul exercises authority among his communities by persuading them to accept his point of view. He does not try to coerce his converts. His persuasion is based on his capacity to convince them, by word and example, that he desires for them only what the gospel requires . . . through the Spirit, God continues to speak and work authoritatively, not through coercion of people's personalities but by convincing their minds of truth and warming their hearts with love so that they freely embrace it. (Paul's Idea of Community)

To Whom Does the Church Belong?

Even though workers had a fatherly responsibility to care for the churches they planted, the church was never the worker's franchise. If one examines all of the letters that Paul wrote to a church, he never once indicates that he had formal possession of it.

Paul never uses imperial metaphors to describe his role in the life of the churches. By contrast, he describes his relationship to them in language drawn from family life rather than from legal, administrative, or political life. The churches Paul planted "belong" to God, to Christ, and to the saints. They only belong to Paul in the sense that children belong to their parents. Paul sees himself as a brother, a father, and a mother—not as a lord, a master, or an owner. Consider the following:

Galatians
- He says the church belongs to Christ twice.
- He says the church belongs to the family of believers once.
- He calls them "brethren" eleven times.
- He describes himself as a mother that has travailed in birth for them.

1 Thessalonians
- He calls the church "brethren" seventeen times.
- He says he dealt with them as a father would his children.
- He says that he was gentle among them as a mother is with her children.

2 Thessalonians
- He calls them "brethren" seven times.

1 Corinthians
- He calls them "brethren" twenty-eight times.
- He says the church belongs to God twice.
- He says the church belongs to Christ once.
- He calls them "his" children.
- He says he belongs to them.
- He says he is a servant to them.

- He uses the imagery of a mother who fed them with milk.
- He says that he is their only father who gave them birth through the gospel.

2 Corinthians
- He calls them "brethren" eight times.
- He calls them "his" children.
- He says he stores up for them as a parent does his children.
- He says he is a father that will present the church to Christ as a chaste virgin.
- He says he is not a lord over them, but a helper of their joy.

Romans
- He calls them "brethren" fourteen times.
- He says they belong to Christ.

Colossians
- He calls them "brethren" two times.

Ephesians
- He calls them "brethren" two times.

Philippians
- He calls them "brethren" eight times.

In closing, NT Professor John Knox perfectly isolates the role and function of the Christian worker saying,

Their primary function was the preaching of the gospel, the proclamation of the event in Palestine with which God was bringing history to a close, the bearing witness to the new

creation in Christ, the calling of men to repentance; but this meant the establishing of churches, and implied the duty and authority of supervision . . . Paul lets us see in his letters not a little of what was involved in this supervisory role of the apostle. It meant, at least for him, a good deal of anxiety and activity. The final and climactic item in a long catalogue of his sufferings as an apostle is his "care for all the churches" (2 Cor. 11:28). He sought to keep in constant, or at least frequent, touch with them. He visited them as often as he was able . . . More often perhaps he sent one of his assistants, men like Timothy, Titus, Silvanus, Epaphras, and others. And frequently, as we have even better reason to know, he wrote letters . . . in the absence of other evidence we are justified in assuming that the general pattern of the relations of other apostles with other churches and of the functions they performed was basically the same. (The Ministry in Historical Perspectives)

How God Produces Workers

Perhaps one of the least understood principles regarding God's work is that itinerant workers *always* emerged from the soil of an existing church. They were those who were given a unique revelation of Christ and of God's eternal purpose in Him. They were people well acquainted with the mystery of God. And they were specially equipped to impart this mystery to others (Eph. 1:9; 3:2-11; Col. 1:24-29). But beyond all of this, a Christian worker learned all of these realities in the context of an existing church where he was a non-leader.[7]

---

[7] Such a person may be raised up by God to be an elder in a local church before he is sent out to the work, but that will not be immediate. Paul and Barnabas were prophets and/or teachers before they were sent out from Antioch (Acts 13:1-2).

In fact, a large part of a worker's preparation for service was to live in the context of an already existing church before he was sent out. Not a Bible study group. Not an institutional church. But a community of believers that met around Jesus Christ alone. It is within this rare setting that the worker both experienced and learned the spiritual and practical realities of Divine life.

First-century workers did not leave the synagogue on Saturday and decide to plant churches on Sunday! They first experienced that which they were sent out to start. This principle is most critical. And aspiring "church planters" who have never lived a day in the context of a first-century styled church should take serious heed to it.

A seminary education cannot equip a person to raise up the church of the living God—nor can any position in an institutional church or Bible study group. Only time spent in a vital expression of the Body of Christ (without an organizational hierarchy) can equip one for such work.

To frame it another way, you cannot produce that which you have never experienced. What is more, the gore and glory—the testing and transforming—the sifting and soaring—the brokenness and beautifying—the exposure and enlargement that Body life affords is absolutely vital for preparing those who are called to God's work.

To blithely launch out to plant a house church without such preparation is sheer presumption. It reflects a profound misunderstanding of God's ways. The exacting nature of the church is designed to prevent would-be workers from becoming clergy-on-wheels who lord over local churches like distant bosses. Living in church life as a *non-leader* is designed to produce brokenness and humility. It is designed to make workers safe to God's people. In God's work, it is not only the method that is important. It is the man that is just as vital. As Watchman Nee says,

We shall do well if we follow in their [the early apostles] steps, but we must realize clearly that even though we adopt apostolic methods, unless we have apostolic consecration, apostolic faith and apostolic power, we shall still fail to see apostolic results. We dare not under-estimate the value of apostolic methods—they are absolutely essential if we are to have apostolic fruits—but we must not overlook the need of apostolic spirituality, and we must not fear apostolic persecution. (The Normal Christian Church Life)

Helpers in the Work

While not all Christians are called to plant churches (1 Cor. 12:29), many are gifted and burdened to assist in the work. We have already seen that Paul had a number of "co-workers" who also planted churches.[8] Yet in addition to these co-

---

[8] There are other men and women who Paul regards as "workers,""co-workers,"and "fellow-workers" in addition to the men Paul trained in Ephesus (including Epaphras). Among them are: Apollos, Barnabas, Silas, Demas, Jesus called Justus, Tryphaena, Tryphosa, Persis, Artemas, Clement, Euodia, Syntyche, Andronicus and Junia. For details, see the following articles in *Dictionary of Paul and His Letters* (Downer's Grove: InterVarsity Press, 1993): "Church Order and Government," pp. 136-137; "Paul and His Coworkers," pp. 183-189.

apostles, Paul had a group of men and women that assisted him in the work.

Some were undoubtedly prophets and teachers; others may not have been. But all of them had a heart for the Lord's work and were willing to serve in whatever capacity they could. Among them are: John Mark, Onesiphorus, Sosthenes, Erastus, Urbanus, Priscilla and Aquila, Crescens, Onesimus, Philemon, Archippus, and Phoebe.

In addition, Peter and Paul often had a supporting team to accommodate them on their trips (Acts 10:23; 11:12; 12:25; 15:2). Remarking on this element, Watchman Nee says,

Some people seem to be appointed by God to build the foundation, while others seem to be appointed to build upon the foundation. Accordingly, some are set up as foremen. I believe we all know what a foundation means. Those who lay a foundation must seek for a rock. They need to find the place and select the proper location for the foundation to be laid. The people who build on it have no such need for locating and deciding on the place to build. They are only responsible to build on wherever the foundation has already been laid . . . With regard to co-workers, that really includes much more than the apostles. As an example from the Bible, we have Aquila and Priscilla who were co-workers. Phoebe too was a fellow worker. (Church Affairs)

Regrettably, some Christians have the misguided idea that being a church planter is the "end-all-be-all" of being a Christian. Such a romanticized notion of being a Christian worker is both tragic and silly.

It is important to understand that just because a person is not called to plant churches does not mean that they are a second-class Christian. Hardly! As stated above, the people that helped Paul had a heart for God's work and were very much involved in it. In fact, the work could not have advanced without them.

The truth is that there are many gifts besides the church planter that are just as valuable in the Body of Christ: Prophets, teachers, evangelists, helpers, exhorters, and those who show mercy are just a few of them.[9]

In the modern institutional church, those who feel "called" of God are given three main options for ministry. You either prepare to be a pastor, a missionary, or a worship leader. But this restricted view of ministry is wholly unbiblical.

In the same way, the NT does not support the idea that there are church planters and then the rest of the Body of Christ. Not at all. There are *many* different giftings that all work together to produce and build up the church.

---

[9] Eph. 4:11ff.; 1 Cor. 12:28ff.; Rom. 12:4ff.

If a man learns without preconceived ideas, he has ears to hear the truth.
  -Clement of Alexandria

CHAPTER 3

THE MASTER PLAN OF CHURCH PLANTING

How were workers prepared for spiritual service in the first century?[1] Watchman Nee once said,

> *Unless the man is right, right methods will be of no use to him or to his work . . . In God's work everything depends on the kind of worker sent out and the kind of convert produced. (The Normal Christian Church Life)*

These words are as profound as they are true. And they go to the heart of *God's* method of raising up workers. To paraphrase, men look for methods, while God looks for men. Many modern Christians become highly enthused when they hear of a fancy new "method" or "scheme" to apply to God's work. But God is far more concerned with *the man* than he is with *the method*. In the words of T. Austin-Sparks:

> *. . . in God's mind, the servant is more than the work. If we are going to come truly into the hands of God for His purpose, then we shall be dealt with by Him in such a way as to continually increase our spiritual measure . . . (The Service of God)*

In the same vein, Roland Allen remarks,

---

[1] This chapter owes a great deal to Gene Edwards' *Overlooked Christianity;* Robert Coleman's, *The Master Plan of Evangelism;* and A.B. Bruce's, *The Training of the Twelve.*

St. Paul's method is not in harmony with the modern Western spirit. We modern teachers from the West are by nature and by training persons of restless activity and boundless self-confidence . . . We are accustomed to do things ourselves for ourselves, to find our own way, to rely upon our own exertions, and we naturally tend to be impatient with others who are less restless and less self-assertive than we are. (Missionary Methods: St. Paul's or Ours?)

The Lord has a unique way of preparing men for His work. It is one that involves transformation. And transformation always includes emptying, suffering, and loss. Put differently, man's way is to search for methods, while God's way is to hand them a cross.

A Root in Eternity

To understand how God prepares itinerant workers we must begin at the starting point of the Christian life: *Eternity past.*

Before creation, there existed only God—a transcendent Community of Three Persons: God the Father, God the Son, and God the Holy Spirit. Based on what we know from the NT, there were three things occurring within the Godhead in the dateless past.

- Divine love.
- Divine fellowship.
- A Divine purpose to enlarge the love and the fellowship to a creature called "man."

Let us unfold that a bit. First, God exchanged Divine love among the three Persons of the Godhead. Within the Trinitarian Community, the Father, the Son, and the Spirit engaged in a Divine dance of passionate and unconditional love one for the other.

God is a Community of perfect, mutual love. And this love is the very fountainhead of the Divine nature (1 John 4:8,16). For this reason, love is the essence of the Christian life. So we can say that the Christian life finds its root in the Godhead in the timeless past (John 13:34-35; 17:23-25; Gal. 5:14; Rom. 13:8-10; 1 Tim. 1:5). Noted theologian Clark Pinnock remarks,

God's essence is spirit—God's character is love . . . the phrase "God is love" refers to the inner life of God . . . the love God has for sinners flows from the love that circulates everlastingly within the Trinity. As Jesus says, "As the Father has loved me, so I have loved you" (John 15:9) . . . John is making reference to a triune love that flows among the persons of the Godhead . . . these persons make up a relational Being, a community of love and mutual indwelling . . . Trinity means that shared life is basic to the nature of God. God is perfect sociality, mutuality, reciprocity and peace. As a circle of loving relationships, God is dynamically alive . . . God's nature is internally complex and consists of a fellowship of three. It is the essence of God's nature to be relational. This is primordial in God and defines who God is. God is a triadic community, not a single, undifferentiated unity. Though beyond our understanding, God is a communion of Persons, and creation is a natural expression of God's life . . . Creation arises from the loving relationships in the Divine nature . . . God is pure ecstasy—each Person exists in loving relationship with the other Persons, and the joyous fellowship spills over into giving life to the creature . . . The Trinity is a fellowship of giving and receiving, and creation is intended to echo mutuality. (Flame of Love)

Note that God must be corporate, for the Scripture says that "God is love" (1 John 4:16). If God is not corporate, there would be no one else for Him to love before creation. As Erich Sauer says,

> *Love is the deepest element of His life, the innermost fount out of which His nature eternally flows forth, the creative centre that begets all His working and ruling. But love is a trinity. Augustine said: "If God is love, then there must be in Him a Lover, a Beloved, and a Spirit of love; for no love is conceivable without a Lover and a Beloved" . . . The Father is the Lover, the Son the Beloved, the Holy Spirit is the Spirit of Love . . . Before the foundation of the whole universe God had been in eternal loving intercourse with His Son. (The Dawn of World Redemption)*

Second, the Divine Community enjoyed eternal fellowship (Prov. 8:22-31; John 1:1-3, 18; 15:26; 17:5). The Father, the Son, and the Spirit mutually experienced what the NT calls *koinonia* (the shared life of the Spirit). *Koinonia* is the essence of the church. The church is a shared life community whose members mutually fellowship with God and with one another (Acts 2:42; 1 Cor. 1:9; 2 Cor. 13:14; 1 John 1:3). Thus we can say that the church finds its origin in the Godhead before time. Theologian Stanley Grenz puts it this way,

> *It is not surprising that ultimately the image of God should focus on "community." As the doctrine of the Trinity asserts, throughout all eternity God is "community," namely the fellowship of Father, Son, and Holy Spirit who comprise the triune God. The creation of humankind in the Divine image, therefore, can mean nothing less than that humans express the relational dynamic of God whose representation we are called to be. Consequently, each person can be related to the image of God only within the context of life in community with others . . . The focus of this present experience, according to the New Testament writers, is the community of Christ. (Theology for the Community of God)*

Third, the members of the Godhead counseled together and conceived an eternal purpose. They shrouded this purpose in a mystery and hid it in the Son until an appointed time (Rom. 16:25; Eph. 1:9-11; 3:3-11). What was this mystery? It was that the Trinitarian Community would one day expand its fellowship to a created race (John 17:20-26; Gal. 6:15; Eph. 2:15; 3:3-6; Col. 1:25-27; 3:11)!

Herein lies the essence of apostolic work. It is to enlarge the circle of Divine love and fellowship. When men and women are brought to Christ and churches are born, the Divine fellowship is expanded. Properly understood, the church is a human community that lives by Divine life and reflects the Divine nature (John 6:57; Gal. 2:20; 2 Pet. 1:4). As Stuart Murray says,

This story is the story of community. The Trinity, God in community, reaches out in creation and in redemption to form a human community to participate in the Divine community . . . Church planting is about establishing new communities of faith. (Church Planting: Laying Foundations)

Stanley Grenz expands the point saying,

. . . the church as community—lifts our conception beyond the activity of God in history to the life of the triune God Himself, which provides the foundation for that activity. The ultimate basis for our understanding of the church lies in its re-lationship to the nature of the triune God Himself . . . Throughout eternity God is Father, Son, and Holy Spirit—the community of love. More specifically, the dynamic of the Trinity is the love shared between the Father and the Son, which is the Holy Spirit. God's purpose is to bring glory to His own triune nature by establishing a reconciled creation in which humans reflect the reality of the Creator. The triune God desires that human beings be brought together into a

fellowship of reconciliation, which not only reflects God's own eternal essence, but actually participates in His nature —2 Pet. 1:4. (Theology of the Community of God)

Charles Chaney adds,

The church and church planting are not trivial afterthought. They were in God's purpose, to use a phrase of Spurgeon's, when this world was in the mind of God, like an oak tree is in the cup of an acorn. (Church Planting at the End of the Twentieth Century)

Consequently, it is within the Eternal Godhead that we locate the headwaters of the Christian life (Divine love expressed), the church (Divine fellowship expressed), and apostolic work (the Divine plan to enlarge the love and fellowship that exist in the Godhead). R. Paul Stevens puts it beautifully,

There was ministry before there was a world, ministry in the being of God. This mutual interanimation, interpenetration, indwelling, covenantal loyalty and othering . . . is the mutual service rendered within God . . . the ministry of the triune God is relational, characterized by love . . . Ministry is God's ministry, arising from the communal life of God, the Father, Son and Spirit ministering love to one another even before there was a world to save . . . All ministry is God's ministry and God continues His own ministry through His people . . . So there was ministry before there was a world, that ministry taking place within God Himself (John 17:5,24). This pre-creation ministry was neither curative nor redemptive. There was nothing broken nor fallen to restore . . . God is not God apart from the way the Father, Son, and Holy Spirit give and receive from one another what they essentially are . . . As Edwin Hui notes, "The three persons of the Trinity [are] 'being into one another'—drawn to the other, contained in the other, interpenetrating each other by drawing life from and pouring life to each other—as the communion of love. (The Abolition of the Laity)

A Conception in Nazareth

When God created the universe, He wove deep into its fabric a series of pictures and symbols that would reflect the mystery of His timeless purpose. Each of the six days of creation typifies God's eternal purpose—a purpose that is bound up with Christ and His beloved kingdom community, the church. Later, God chose a specific nation (Israel) to prefigure and foreshadow the Christian life, the church, and apostolic work.

Finally, at an appointed time the Son of God stepped out of the heavenly portals of glory and became a man. Born in Bethlehem and raised in Nazareth, Jesus Christ embodied God's eternal thought for humanity. (This is the meaning of the Lord's oft-used title, "Son of Man.")

With the advent of the Lord Jesus, what had its root in eternity past was conceived in a carpenter's shop in the ill-reputed town of Nazareth (John 1:46). It was in that carpenter's shop that God the Father taught Jesus three things (Luke 2:40,49,52; 4:16):

- To walk in Divine love.
- To fellowship with God.
- To enlarge the Divine love and fellowship to others.

First, the Father taught His Son how to live by Divine love (John 5:19-20,26,30; 7:16; 8:26,28; 10:37-38; 12:49-50; 14:10). The Christian life is a life lived by Divine life.

The Son showed forth God's idea for man. In God's thought, man is a God-created being that lives by Divine life and expresses Divine love. The Son, therefore, brought to the earth the unconditional love He knew before His incarnation. In this way, Jesus Christ expressed the image of God as a man. He revealed to men and angels how a human being could live by Divine life. Jesus Christ lived the Christian life by means of His Father's life, and the hallmark of that life is love (John 6:57). To quote Ian Thomas, "It takes God to be a man."[2]

Second, the Father taught the Son how to fellowship with Him as a man. In the days of His flesh, the Lord Jesus learned to fellowship with His Father internally. Consequently, within our Lord's inner parts resided the seeds of the church. Just as Eve lay in the bosom of Adam before her appearance, so the church lay within the bosom of the Son before He gave birth to her (Gen. 2:18-24; Eph. 5:25-32).

As a man, Jesus Christ continued the Divine *koinonia* that He had once known in eternity past. Within our Lord's bosom, humanity had fellowship with Divinity. For the first time a human being was brought into vital participation with the Divine Community. In this way, Jesus Christ incarnated God's eternal purpose for man. As theologian Stanley Grenz says,

> *Jesus displays the relationship of the Son to the Father. As a result, the one who referred to God as His own Father is none other than the eternal Son of the Father . . . [He is the] beloved Son of the Father who gives back to the Father the love He receives . . . The relationship Jesus enjoyed with Abba is the fellowship that characterizes the interaction*

---

[2] Incidentally, the way that most modern believers are taught to live the Christian life is a poor fit to the way that Christ demonstrated how to live it. Jesus did not try to be good; He lived by the indwelling life of His Father.

between the Father and the Son in the eternal Divine life. As the Divine Son, Jesus lives in intimate community with the Father . . . Jesus, therefore, reveals to us the fellowship—the community—of the triune God . . . Jesus is indeed Deity, for He shares with the Father who sent Him the Divine essence—love—which is the Spirit of the Father and the Son. (Theology for the Community of God)

Third, the Father trained the Son how to be the first apostolic worker (John 4:34; 9:4; Heb. 3:1). Jesus learned from His Father how to build His church, the very organism that He would later give His life for (Matt. 16:18; Eph. 5:25).

Amazingly, Jesus did not learn how to serve His Father and build the church at the hands of religious specialists. The would-be scribes of His day formally studied the Hebrew Scriptures, the oral traditions, and the rabbinical commentaries under tutors. The would-be priests went off to master the intricacies of their sacred trade. By contrast, Jesus learned how to be the first Christian worker as a manual laborer in a lowly carpenter shop.

Jesus knew no seminary, no human tutors, nor any academic program. Instead, He learned to fellowship with His Father, love His Father, obey His Father, and receive His Father's doctrine amid the splinters and sawdust that lay amid a "layman's" workplace. (In this connection, the way that men are trained for the so-called "ministry" today is in complete dissonance with God's chosen way of training men for His work.)

Therefore, what had its root within the Godhead in eternity past was conceived in the Nazarene carpenter. The Christian life, the church, and apostolic work were all experienced within the God-man, Jesus of Nazareth.

An Embryo in Galilee

As arresting as it sounds, it took the Father approximately thirty years to train His Son to be the first apostolic worker. The Lord Jesus did not begin His earthly ministry until He was empowered by the Spirit at about age thirty (Luke 3:22-23). This occurred at His baptism in the Jordan River (Matt. 3:16-17). Christ did no preaching, teaching, or healing until He was sent by His Father at that time (Luke 4:1,16-18).

Thus the Father *called* Jesus Christ, *prepared* Him for thirty years, and finally *sent* Him to accomplish His work.[3] As we will shortly see, being *called, prepared,* and *sent* is an unbroken spiritual principle that consistently runs throughout the saga of the first-century church.

A word should be given about calling and sending. A call to the work is a call to Divine service, not to meet a human need. It is a call to minister unto the Lord and to be devoted to Him. A call should be followed by a sending.

All genuine Christians workers are sent. This implies that they do not take initiative in God's work. Nor do they take it in their own hands. Those who take up God's work who are not sent are volunteers. And God knows no volunteers when it comes to *His* work. As Watchman Nee says,

> . . . *The special position occupied by apostles is obvious to any reader of the New Testament. They were specially commissioned by God to found churches through the preaching of the gospel, to bring revelation from God to His people, to give decisions in matters pertaining to doctrine and*

---

[3] Granted, following His earthly ministry, our Lord accomplished His greatest work at Calvary. But because the scope of this piece is our Lord's earthly life and ministry, we will not deal with His atoning work—which is unique to Him alone.

government, and to edify the saints and distribute the gifts . . . they have a special calling and special commission . . . apostleship is not based on human qualification but on Divine commission. It takes more than mere gift and ability to constitute men apostles; it takes nothing less than God Himself, God's will and God's call. (The Normal Christian Church Life)

Significantly, the word "apostle" in the Greek literally means "one who is *sent*." The book of Hebrews tells us that Jesus Christ was a sent one (Heb. 3:1). Consider how conscious the Lord was of His own sending:[4]

"My food," said Jesus, "is to do the will of him who SENT me and to finish his work." (John 4:34)

He who does not honor the Son does not honor the Father, who SENT him. (John 5:23)

Whoever hears my word and believes him who SENT me has eternal life . . . (John 5:24)

. . . I seek not to please myself but him who SENT me. (John 5:30)

. . . For the very work that the Father has given me to finish, and which I am doing, testifies that the Father has SENT me. (John 5:36)

And the Father who SENT me has himself testified concerning me. (John 5:37)

. . . You do not believe the one he SENT. (John 5:38)

---

[4] The following passages come from the first six chapters of John's Gospel (NIV). Many more examples can be multiplied throughout that Gospel.

. . . The work of God is this: to believe in the one he has SENT. (John 6:29)

For I have come down from heaven not to do my will but to do the will of him who SENT me. (John 6:38)

And this is the will of him who SENT me . . . (John 6:39)

No one can come to me unless the Father who SENT me draws him . . . (John 6:44)

Just as the living Father SENT me . . . (John 6:57)

When God sends someone to His work, God Himself is being sent as well. As R. Paul Stevens says,

Not only does the Father send the Son, and the Father and Son send the Spirit, but the Father, Son and Spirit send the church into the world. Mission is the sending of God from first to last . . . God becomes not only the Sender but simultaneously the One who is sent . . . Every sending of one Person results in the presence of the Other. So God is not only the One sent but is the content of the sending "for in every Person of the Deity God works in His entirety." Mission is God's own going forth . . . He is Sender, Sent and Sending . . . In Jesus God is both the Sender and the One sent, both the revealer and the revelation. (The Abolition of the Laity)

The sending of the Son holds tremendous significance for all who are sent to God's work today. If Jesus, the first worker was sent, how much more should all workers after Him be sent? As Watchman Nee has said of the first-century apostles,

It was the Lordship of Christ that claimed their service, and it was on His authority alone that they went forth. Their call was a spiritual call, no natural factor entered into it. It was

the Holy Spirit who said, "Separate me Barnabas and Saul for the work whereunto I have called them." All spiritual work must begin with the Spirit's call; all Divine work must be divinely initiated. The plan conceived for the work may be splendid, the reason adequate, the need urgent, and the man chosen to carry it out may be eminently suitable; but if the Holy Spirit has not said, "Separate me that man for the work to which I have called him," he can never be an apostle . . . The tragedy in Christian work today is that so many workers have simply gone out, they have not been sent. It is Divine commission that constitutes the call to Divine work. Personal desire, friendly persuasions, the advice of one's elders and the urge of opportunity—all these are factors on the natural plane, and they can never take the place of a spiritual call . . . A Divine call gives God His rightful place, for it recognizes Him as the Originator of the work. (The Normal Christian Church Life)

The call to the work is intensely personal. But the sending is corporate. A worker will have a personal revelation of God's calling on his life. And it is vital that he is absolutely *sure* of this calling. (If a person is unsure of his calling, he *will* create problems in the work.) A worker's calling should be confirmed by representative members of the Body of Christ who send him out. This principle keeps workers from being free-lancing lone-rangers in God's work. As David Shenk and Ervin Stutzman point out,

One's personal sense of call must be confirmed by the church. Otherwise, two serious problems may arise. First, it might be that the aspiring church planter has ulterior motives. Perhaps the idea to plant a church is of one's own making, and not from the Lord. If the church planting ministry is not God's appointment, the church planter may become quickly discouraged and the effort will not bear lasting fruit. The second problem is that the church planter needs a praying com-

munity to provide encouragement. If the planter is a loner, long-term survival is doubtful. Paul returned to Antioch occasionally for refreshment and retreat. All church planters deserve and need that same kind of home church support. (Creating Communities of the Kingdom)

This brings us to the Twelve. Shortly after Jesus began His earthly ministry, He called twelve men (Luke 6:13). The Lord *called* these men to His work (Matt. 4:19-21; 9:9; Mark 1:19-21; Luke 6:13), *prepared* them for it, and finally *sent* them to carry it out (Mark 3:13-14). As the Father called, prepared, and sent the Son—the Son called, prepared, and sent the Twelve (John 17:18).

How did the Lord Jesus prepare the Twelve after He called them? The short answer is that He prepared them the same way His Father prepared Him. There were essentially three leading elements in the Son's training of the Twelve. And they run parallel with what happened in both Nazareth and eternity past:

- He taught them how to walk in Divine love.
- He taught them how to fellowship with God.
- He taught them how to expand the Divine love and fellowship to others.

First, Christ trained the Twelve how to live by Divine love, which is the essence of the Christian life. The essential ingredient in this training lay in the words:

He appointed twelve—designating them apostles—that THEY MIGHT BE WITH HIM. (Mark 3:14)

The Twelve lived with the Son! They consistently watched Him relate to His indwelling Father. They beheld the incomparable manner in which He denied Himself and poured His life out for others. They marveled at His peerless words, awed at His matchless compassion, observed His sagacious handling of criticism, studied His gracious responses to persecution, and scrutinized His heart-felt praying. As A.B. Bruce says,

In the training of the twelve for the work of apostleship, hearing and seeing the words and works of Christ necessarily occupied an important place. Eye and ear witnessing of the facts of an unparalleled life was an indispensable preparation for future witness-bearing. (The Training of the Twelve)

In short, the Twelve watched a man live by Divine life. And this "watching" did not take place from the sidelines. It happened in the heart of the playing field as the Twelve *lived* in the presence of the Son of God. In this way, Jesus' mode of pedagogy represents a dramatic break with today's data-transfer model of teaching where information is sterilely passed from one notebook to another. (The former mode yields transformed disciples while the latter breeds isolated consumers of mental information. But this is another discussion.)

Second, Jesus introduced the Twelve to the life of the church. That is, they learned to fellowship with Jesus and with one another in informal settings. They sat at His feet and listened to His word in homes, on seashores, along dusty roads, on mountain tops, and around campfires—asking Him questions and responding to His inquiries (Mark 4:10,34; 7:17; Luke 8:9; 9:18; 11:1; John 6:3; 9:2). The Twelve consistently enjoyed table fellowship with one other while breaking bread with the Son of God in their midst (Matt. 26:26; Luke 24:41-43).

Interestingly, these activities are the chief features of the first church that would be born a few years afterward (Acts 2:42). Hence, the primitive simplicity that the Twelve enjoyed with Jesus in Galilee constituted the embryo of the church. It was a foreshadowing of what was to come: Humanity participating in the fellowship of Divinity with Christ as Head!

Third, the Lord trained the Twelve to be workers. What did that training consist of? It certainly was not what natural minds would suspect. Contrary to the modern day practice of preparing men for "the ministry," the Twelve did very little spiritual service while Jesus was on earth.

Granted, they had two trial missions that seemingly lasted only a few weeks (Mark 6:7ff.; Luke 10:1ff.). Subsequently, they returned and reported on their experience to receive the Lord's feedback (Mark 6:30; Luke 9:10; 10:17ff.). However, the bulk of the Twelve's activities consisted of mundane tasks like distributing food to hungry multitudes, managing housing arrangements for the Lord's itinerant ministry, baptizing new converts, and preparing food for their journeys.

Jesus taught the Twelve how to fulfill God's work by *modeling* it before them daily. By His example, He showed them the more practical matters of prayer, ministry, self-denial, healing, showing compassion, handling conflict, and addressing questions. But the most important part of their training for service lay in their experience of corporate life under the Lord's Headship. Robert Coleman remarks,

Everything He [Jesus] did and said was motivated by this consuming passion. His life was simply the revelation in time of God's eternal purpose to save for Himself a people. Supremely this is what the disciples needed to learn, not in theory, but in practice. And they saw it practiced before them in many ways every day. (The Master Plan of Evangelism)

Note that the Twelve not only lived with Jesus; they lived with one another. And through their shared community-life, the Twelve were terrifically exposed. The carnality lurking in the shadows was made manifest as the disciples' wills collided. The dark side of their personalities was laid bare as the Twelve chafed against each other (Matt. 8:25-26; 17:19-20; Mark 6:52; 10:13-14, 35-37,41; 14:29-30; 16:14; Luke 9:46,54; 22:24).

It was in that three-year period of living in an intense, shared-life community with Jesus Christ as Center that the Twelve were exposed, tried, and broken. It was within that corporate context that they learned the priceless lessons of relatedness, forbearance, patience, longsuffering, humility, forgiveness, and compassion. (Incidentally, such lessons exact an obscenely high price.) Yet it was the magnificent texture of that experience that eventually qualified the Twelve to be useful in the Master's hands. In short, the Galilean embryo of the church became the Divine training ground for the Twelve. Again, Robert Coleman writes,

Amazing as it may seem, all Jesus did to teach these men His way was to draw them close to Himself. He was his own school and curriculum . . . The time which Jesus invested in these few disciples was so much more by comparison to that given to others that it can only be regarded as a deliberate strategy. He actually spent more time with His disciples than with everybody else in the world put together. He ate with them, slept with them, and talked with them for the most part of His entire active ministry . . . One must not overlook that even while Jesus was ministering to others, the disciples were always there with Him. Whether He addressed the multitudes that pressed on him, conversed with the scribes and Pharisees which sought to ensnare Him, or spoke to some lonely beggar along the road, the disciples were close at hand to observe and to learn . . . Without any fanfare and unnoticed by the world, Jesus was saying that He had been training men to be His witnesses after He had gone, and His method of doing it was simply by being "with them." (The Master Plan of Evangelism)

A Birth in Jerusalem

After three years of living with and beholding the Son of God, the Twelve were *sent* by Jesus to begin their ministry of planting churches (Matt. 28:18-20; John 20:21). The twelve *disciples* had in reality become the twelve *apostles*—"sent ones."

After His resurrection, Christ breathed into the Twelve the very life that indwelt Him. And twelve uneducated Galileans possessed an indwelling Lord (John 20:22). Once Christ had fully prepared the Twelve, He left them on their own (John 14:28). Yet He really did not leave them alone. He rather abandoned them to the Holy Spirit (John 16:7). Hence, the Christ who they had once fellowshipped with in person had now come into them by the Spirit (John 14:16-18; 16:13-16). Just as Jesus Christ lived by an indwelling Father, the Twelve began to live by an indwelling Son. The passage had moved from the Father to the Son to the Twelve (John 17:18; 20:21).

On the day of Pentecost the church was birthed in Jerusalem and three thousand souls were quickly added to her. The baton had now passed into the hands of the Twelve. They raised up the Jerusalem assembly by declaring Jesus Christ to the unregenerate and showing them how to live by His indwelling life.

Galilee had expanded into Jerusalem. And the Twelve had passed on to the saints in Jerusalem the same fellowship they had known with the Son of God . . . which was the same fellowship that the Son had known with His Father on earth as well as before creation (Acts 4:20; 1 John 1:1-3). The church—the expanded community of Divine love and fellowship—was born! Theologian Clark Pinnock writes,

Community is also central to the purpose of God because it allows the relationality of the triune life to be reflected in the created order . . . The Spirit is central for ecclesiology because He is the source of fellowship among humans in history and the bond of love between Father and Son in eternity . . . . The church is meant to resemble the triune life by being itself a place of reciprocity and self-giving. The fellowship that we have with one another is related ultimately to our fellowship with Father and Son (1 John 1:3) . . . Fellowship refers to Divine life and to community life, because the community is meant to reflect the community of the Trinity, which is the ontological basis of the church. (Flame of Love)

R. Paul Stevens puts it this way:

God who is community of Father, Son, and Spirit has created a community that expresses God's love life on earth. (The Abolition of the Laity)

Stanley Grenz sharpens the point saying,

The church reflects God's character in that it lives as a genuine community—lives in love—for as the community of love the church shows the nature of the triune God . . . the community of love which the church is called to be is no ordinary reality. The fellowship we share with each other is not merely that of a common experience or a common narrative, as important as these are. Our fellowship is nothing less than our common participation in the Divine communion between the Father and the Son mediated by the Holy Spirit . . . because God is a social reality, it is only in relationship—in community—that we are able to reflect the

*Divine nature. Hence, we can only exemplify the Divine
image within the context of community, specifically, the
community of the people who together acknowledge the
lordship of Jesus the Christ. (Theology for the Community of
God)*

Over the next eight years in the church at Jerusalem, God
began to secure a number of men for His work. These men
were exposed, broken, tried, and unwittingly trained in the
corporate context of Body life. And they began to surface as
fit vessels in the Lord's hands. Among this company were
James (the Lord's brother), Stephen, Philip, Agabus, Silas,
Judas, and Barnabas. These men emerge on the stage of the
first-century drama as men who engaged in itinerant ministry.
(Barnabas, Silas, and James would later become itinerant
workers.)

Notwithstanding, all of these men did not engage in
Christian work until they first received years of experience in
the church at Jerusalem. Thus the trek that these seven men
walked mapped perfectly with that of the Twelve in Galilee.

A Walk in the Aegean World

What began inside the Godhead in eternity past was
conceived within one Man in Nazareth. It developed as an
embryo within a group of twelve men in Galilee. And it was
born in the midst of three thousand converts in Jerusalem.
This same principle continues unbroken throughout the pages
of the NT. Approximately ten years after his conversion, Paul
of Tarsus was sent out by the Holy Spirit along with Barnabas
to the work of planting churches.

However, as was the case with all workers who had
preceded them, Paul and Barnabas had spent a considerable
amount of time learning Christ in the context of church life.

This experience preceded their "being sent" to itinerant work. (Before they were sent, Barnabas had spent about eleven years in the Jerusalem assembly. Paul had spent about five years in the Antioch assembly.)[5] Furthermore, as Barnabas received training by living with and watching the Twelve in Jerusalem, Paul received training by living with and watching Barnabas in Antioch.[6] E. Stanley Jones writes,

> . . . *Barnabas felt the urge to get Saul back into the stream of Christian life and action. It was the greatest thing he ever did, for Paul left to Tarsus and Arabia would have withered as an ascetic. Barnabas brought him to Antioch and Antioch made Paul. Made him "into" Paul, for it was after his contact with Antioch that Saul became Paul. (The Reconstruction of the Church—On What Pattern?)*

Both Paul and Barnabas were clearly *called* by God to His work. Consider Paul's testimony about himself:

> *Paul, an apostle (not sent from men, nor through the agency of man, but through Jesus Christ, and God the Father, who raised Him from the dead) . . . (Gal. 1:1)*

---

[5] In Antioch, Paul quickly matured to be a prophet/teacher along with Barnabas (Acts 13:1). Apostles, therefore, are first brothers. They then grow to manifest their gift as prophets, teachers, evangelists, etc. They are then sent out to use their gift to plant churches. Not all prophets, teachers, and evangelists ever become apostles. But apostles are often prophets, teachers, and/or evangelists before they are sent.

[6] This seems clear from the fact that the more experienced Barnabas searched for Saul in Tarsus and brought him to Antioch to help with the work there (Acts 11:25ff.). Also, Luke makes clear by his wording that Barnabas took the lead role above Paul until the two men got to Paphos (Acts 13:13, 42-43, et al.). Before this point, Luke always mentions Barnabas' name ahead of Paul's; afterwards, he always says "Paul and Barnabas." See F.F. Bruce, *The Pauline Circle* (Grand Rapids: Eerdmans, 1985), pp. 18-19; Watchman Nee, *Church Affairs* (New York: Christian Fellowship Publishers, 1982), pp. 135-141.

Paul, an apostle of Christ Jesus, by the will of God. (Eph. 1:1; Col. 1:1)

Paul, an apostle of Christ Jesus, by the command of God. (1 Tim. 1:1)

I was appointed . . . an apostle. (2 Tim. 1:11)

I was appointed . . . an apostle. (1 Tim. 2:7)

Consider the testimony about Barnabas concerning his apostolic calling:

So Paul and Barnabas spent considerable time there, speaking boldly for the Lord, who confirmed the message of his grace by enabling them to do miraculous signs and wonders. The people of the city were divided; some sided with the Jews, others with the APOSTLES. (Acts 14:3-4)

But when the APOSTLES Barnabas and Paul heard of this, they tore their clothes and rushed out into the crowd, shouting. (Acts 14:14)

James, Peter and John, those reputed to be pillars, gave me and Barnabas the right hand of fellowship when they recognized the grace given to me. They agreed that WE SHOULD GO TO THE GENTILES, and they to the Jews. (Gal. 2:9)

Don't we have the right to take a believing wife along with us, as do THE OTHER APOSTLES and the Lord's brothers and Cephas? Or is it only I and Barnabas who must work for a living? (1 Cor. 9:5-6)

The words "by the will of God," "by the command of God," "through Jesus Christ and God the Father," "appointed," and "go to" have to do with Divine sending and commissioning.

Paul and Barnabas stand in a long lineage of itinerant workers who were called, prepared, and then sent. Interestingly, just as the *Father* trained and sent the Son . . . and the *Son* trained and sent the Twelve . . . it was the *Spirit* who trained and sent Paul and Barnabas (Acts 13:4).

But this principle did not end with these two men. After he was sent out, Paul accomplished the following familiar activities: He modeled the Christian life to his new converts (1 Cor. 4:16; 11:1; 2 Thess. 3:7-9), he raised up churches in Galatia, Macedonia, Achaia, and Asia Minor (Acts 13-20), and he trained other called men to be workers (Acts 20:1-4; 1 Cor. 4:17; 1 Tim. 1:2; 2 Tim. 2:1-2).

Paul trained men in Ephesus the same way that Jesus trained the Twelve in Galilee. David Shenk and Ervin Stutzman state it beautifully,

Paul's strategy for leadership training is not unlike that of Jesus. At the beginning of His ministry, Jesus invested much time in prayer, then called twelve men whom he commissioned to be apostles. For the next three years, Jesus used the same training approaches for his disciples as Paul later used for those whom he was training. Jesus modeled leadership. He provided opportunities for the apostles and for many other disciples, as well, to practice ministry. He taught them the nature of the kingdom. He also provided field trips for them, including several journeys into Gentile communities where they could see firsthand the cross-cultural relevance of the gospel of the kingdom. Jesus was aware that he could not teach everyone with equal intensity. Yet Jesus had a mission—the establishment of the church in such a way that it would be equipped to extend to the ends of the earth. Since He Himself could not go to the ends of the earth, He focused on training twelve leaders . . . Jesus faithfully trained leaders who took the gospel into areas which he could never have reached in a single lifetime. Every church planter should do the same. Not only is he commissioned to plant a church, but also to train men and women in apostolic ministry to go out from the congregation to extend the gospel in regions beyond. This needs to be a foundational commitment of every church planter: plant churches and train others to do the same. (Creating Communities of the Kingdom)

Just as the men that Jesus trained learned by "being with" and "watching" Him, the men that Paul trained learned in the same manner. Again, David Shenk and Ervin Stutzman write,

For several years, Timothy learned from Paul by watching him work and by assisting him in his work. He was with Paul in Philippi when they met with Lydia and the women at the river . . . He witnessed Paul being beaten and imprisoned, and he saw God's miraculous intervention in the earthquake . . . In all these experiences Timothy watched Paul and worked with him. He "saw" and "did" ministry in partnership with Paul not only in Philippi, but in subsequent church planting in other cities. (Creating Communities of the Kingdom)

As was the case in his own life, the men that Paul trained were: 1) *Called* by God, 2) *Prepared* in the context of church life, and 3) Later *sent* through the Spirit by Paul himself (Acts 16:1-3; 19:22; 1 Cor. 4:17; 1 Thess. 3:1-2). Thus the Divine principle of being called, prepared, and sent unshakably holds throughout the entire NT.

No solution, no matter how creative or highpowered, can succeed if you have defined the problem incorrectly. Put differently: more important than giving the right answers is asking the right questions . . . Simply changing the materials, programs, and activities is not enough. We must change how we perceive the church, how we see God expressing Himself in the world through the church, and how we do church.
-William A. Beckham

CHAPTER 4

THE MODERN HOUSE CHURCH MOVEMENT

We live in a day where there exists a "primitive church phenomenon." Countless Christians around the globe are seeing afresh that the modern practice of "church" is Biblically groundless and spiritually ineffective. As a result, many have left the institutional church and have returned to the first-century practice of meeting in homes without a clergy.

Some have dubbed this phenomenon "the house church movement." But this is a misnomer for two reasons. First, it places the emphasis on the wrong thing—the house. Granted, the location of the church meeting is not without significance. But what God is after goes far beyond where His people meet. To put it bluntly, there is nothing inherently magical about meeting in a house. While gathering in homes is better than gathering in basilicas, it is not the hallmark of the church.

Secondly, the word "movement" conveys a unified motion among a group of people. Those who meet in homes contain every stripe of Christian and represent every doctrinal pedigree. Consequently, there exists no monolithic movement that reflects all house churches. For these reasons, the phrase "house church movement" is misleading. House churches gather for different reasons and focus on different themes. And these differences are so great that they place many house churches galaxies apart.

Some Sub-Cultures of House Church

Most of the groups that fly under the flag of "house church" or "NT church" fit neatly into one of the following categories:

The Glorified Bible Study. This brand of house church is typically chaired by an ex-clergyman or aspiring Bible teacher. This person usually facilitates a round-table discussion of the Scriptures. Meetings are dominated by Bible expositions which often descend into fruitless debates. In the glorified Bible study, those members who are not theologically inclined have a rather thin participation. Whether he recognizes it or not, the person facilitating the Bible study is in charge of the church.

The Special Interest Group. These home groups make their focal point for assembling a common interest like home school, home birth, the keeping of Jewish feasts, a particular eschatological view, a pro forma pattern of church service, organic farming, personal prophecy, "Holy Ghost laughter," social justice, or some other issue, fad, or thing—even "house church" itself!

The Personality Cult. Members of these groups center their universe around a gifted man or woman. It may be a dead apostle whose writings act as the exclusive medium for the group's identity, beliefs, and practices. More often, the object of attention is a Christian leader who founds the church and perpetually stays resident within it. While the gifted personality often has a genuine desire to see the Body build *itself* up, his mere presence obstructs this spiritual dynamic. He is typically blind to the fact that he has unwittingly fostered an unhealthy dependence upon himself. Therefore, he is the son of the modern pastor.

The Bless-Me-Club. At bottom, this is a narcissistic community—a spiritual ghetto. The meetings are insular and highly charismatic. The group functions as a spiritual fueling station for burned out Christians in need of an emotional fix. Churches of this ilk are dominated by navel-gazing individualists. Thus its members typically bail-out whenever the group faces a rough thicket. So when conflict or dry spells occur, those who were most zealous about "house church" end up being lured back to the polish and flair of the program-driven religious system.

The Socially Amorphous Party. These home groups are typically comprised of four to eight people who nebulously meet in a living room to chat over tea and cookies. They rarely attain critical mass due to a lack of vision and purpose. They like to speak bulbously about Jesus being present whenever "two or three are gathered together." However, they usually fold before they even begin to understand why they exist. If they do not fold, their meetings become progressively sterile as the years roll by.

The Disgruntled Malcontent Society. Comprised of ex-church derelicts and recycled Christians, these groups happily assemble to lick their wounds and slam the "spiritually abusive" institutional church. Their meetings are permeated with an atmosphere of pessimism, cynicism, and veiled bitterness. Tragically, after the members tire of attacking the organized church, they begin to chew one another up. Thus they find themselves taken by the same spirit they set out to oppose. This form of house church attracts Christians who are deeply wounded and have never learned to trust others.

The Unwritten Liturgy Driven Church. These groups clearly stand outside the stream of institutional Christianity. But they often do not meet in a home. Many gather in a rented building or a "meeting hall." The dominating weakness of their gatherings is the lurking presence of an unwritten liturgy. The ironclad liturgy, which is practiced perfunctorily every week, is never questioned or changed. In fact, if the order of worship is broken in any way, the leadership of the church will call the violators on the carpet to reprove them for their irreverence!

All of the aforementioned groups happily sail under the banner of "house church" or "NT church." Yet they all fall short of the Scriptural idea of church. By NT standards, *a church* is a group of Christians that gathers unto, by, and for the Lord Jesus Christ alone. It is an assembly of believers who are fiercely committed to Christ's full expression in their community. Jesus Christ is the life-blood of the church. He is the Center. He is the Circumference. He is the Content. He is the Focus. He is the sole gathering point of the church.

The saints who gather as *a church* are consumed with Jesus Christ and nothing else. Their goal is to make Him visible in their community. Their hallmark is their growing knowledge of the Lord. And their testimony is an unmistakable love for one another. House churches that are not characterized by these spiritual features not only miss a step, but they dance the wrong dance.

A genuine church is neither issue-centered, person-centered, nor doctrine-centered. It is Christ-centered! The church exists for one purpose and one purpose alone: The unveiling of the centrality and supremacy of her Lord! In fact, in God's view the church is a Person, not a structure. It is Jesus Christ in corporate human expression (Acts 2:47; 5:14; 9:4; 11:24; 1 Cor. 12:12).

The Short Shelf-Life of a House Church

It is quite telling to note that many modern house churches disintegrate over a brief time span. The typical house church has an average life span of six months to four years.

Within this six-to-four window, the church usually dissolves due to an irreconcilable split or an unresolved crisis. (The crisis is usually rooted in a high-drama power struggle, a sustained bickering over hobby-horse theology, or an unwillingness to forebear with intractable personalities.)

If the group manages to hold together through the thrall of such conflict, it usually drifts toward a scaled down, "small-is-beautiful" version of the institutional church. That is, someone from within the group will devolve into the near equivalent of a modern pastor.

This person may not be dubbed "the pastor." And he may not act like an authority-monger. But he will function like a professional cleric, and the saints will grow to over-depend upon him.

The other likely result is that a group of men who tag themselves "elders" will surface and rule the church in oligarchical fashion—running roughshod over everyone else's sensibilities. In these respects, scores of modern house churches have failed to rid themselves of the old leaven of authoritarianism.

Granted, there are house churches that push past the four-year mark. But they are rare. It is still rarer to find a house church that has been in existence for over ten years. House churches that have been extant over twenty years are an endangered species. And house churches that have over twenty years of mileage are exotically scarce.

In short, when Jesus Christ is not the center of a house church, the only fuel that can drive it is a fascinating issue, a charismatic personality, or a nifty doctrine. But all of these fuels yield low mileage. And when they run dry, the group collapses.

A fellowship of believers can only be held together in any beneficial way when a continual encounter with the Lord Jesus becomes the dominating element. At bottom, if Christ is not the glue of a non-institutional church, its meetings will become shallow, colorless, and eventually unsustainable.

The Psalmist once uttered, *"If the foundations be destroyed, what can the righteous do?"* (Psalms. 11:3). Why have so many house churches bitten the dust? Most often it is because they were not founded upon a revelation of the Lord Jesus Christ. Instead, they were founded upon something less.

There are a raft of things today that Christians assemble around—even noble things that have something to do with Christ. The following "things" have taken center stage in most modern house churches in the West:

- Calvinism ("the doctrines of grace").
- Some end-time theology (usually preterism, post-millenialism, or pre-tribulationalism).
- Spiritual gifts.
- "Holy Ghost laughter" and being "slain in the Spirit."
- Personal prophecy.
- Faith Healing.
- Home Schooling.
- Home Birthing.
- Some political viewpoint.
- Social justice and helping the poor.
- Any-man's doctrine (meaning, the group exists to debate various doctrines from the Bible).
- House churching.
- Social fellowship ("hanging out").
- The doctrine of ultimate reconciliation or universalism (even the devil gets saved in the end).

- Eternal security.
- An academic Bible study.
- Evangelism.
- Personal holiness.
- Spiritual warfare.
- Health and nutrition.

All of these "things" are the glue that holds such groups together. But there is a colossal difference between meeting around some "thing" about the Lord and meeting around the Lord Himself! There is a vast ocean between meeting around an "it" and meeting around "Him"!

If you were to read your NT with an eye for discovering how the early churches were formed, you would find that they were solidly built upon the unshakable revelation of Jesus Christ (Matt. 16:16-18). All the churches that Paul planted were built upon this revelation (1 Cor. 3:11). And out of this mighty unveiling of Christ, churches spontaneously issued forth. (Note that the apostolic declaration of Jesus Christ has community forming properties.)

Because the church is founded upon the Lord Jesus Christ, it can survive under the most intense pressure and testing (1 Cor. 3:6-15). The winds may blow brutally and the floods fall fiercely, but the house will stand because it is founded upon a Rock (Matt. 7:24-27; Luke 6:46-48). Put another way, Jesus Christ is the only unmovable foundation upon which God's people may rightfully gather.

Those Christians who are seeking to serve God without the sturdy props of human hierarchy must build their community life upon Jesus Christ. If they do not, their chances of surviving are close to nil.

The First Wave of House Church

The so-called "house church movement" is suffering severely because of a colossal failure to return to first principles. God has His own particular way of raising up a glorious Bride for His Son. It is an ancient way that begins in the Person of God Himself when He sent His Son, the first apostolic worker, to "build His church" (John 4:34; Matt. 16:18; Eph. 5:27).

Tragically, many "house church" folk reject the ministry of the itinerant worker. The reason for this is partly historical. In the late 1960s and early 1970s the United States saw its first move of God outside the religious system. Countless converts were made during this time period. Many of them began to meet in the primitive simplicity of homes without a clergy. Most of these budding "house churches" were populated with young people.

Consequently, many clerical leaders felt it was their task to bring stability to the growing movement. A good number of these men left their clerical positions on Sunday and instantly rose to become leaders of the new movement on Monday.

In a very short period of time, these men introduced to these simple groups a form of discipleship that eventually squeezed from them all semblance of life. While their motives were noble, they did untold damage to a genuine move of God. The young converts who once knew no human headship were used to spawn international movements (which eventually became full-fledged denominations) built on legalism and authoritarianism. The scores of living, breathing house churches and Christian communities that thrived were swallowed up by these movements. Christian lives were shipwrecked on the rock of a perverted doctrine of authority. The work of God was choked by the hands of men.

How could this happen? Simple. These leaders knew nothing of God's way of raising up workers. They had never spent a day in church life as non-leaders. Neither were they trained nor sent.

The Second Wave of House Church

During the late 1980s and early 1990s this country witnessed its second stirring outside the organized church. It was at this time that the phrase "house church movement" was born. Unlike the earlier move of God, most of the people in the second movement were not youth, but middle-aged adults. Few of them were new converts. Most were Christians who were disaffected with the institutional church. So they left their sacred buildings. They dumped their pastors. And they began to gather in homes.

As a reaction to the flaws of the first movement, the second wave of house church folk looked upon any form of itinerant church planting with a suspicious eye. The movement was taken captive by a spirit of absolute egalitarianism that ruled out any need for outside help. The common thinking went like this: "We have no need of church planters. We are all equal in Christ. We have no need of itinerant ministry of any sort. Anyone can start a house church." Sadly, this thinking is still alive today. Yet those who have embraced this idea are ignorant of its origin.

The peril of the first "house church movement" was the fact that God's people did not exercise discernment in welcoming itinerant ministers. They embraced a group of spiritual leaders who were untested. None of them spent any time being trained within the context of an existing house church. Instead, these ministers retained their clerical statuses. They simply switched their sphere of ministry from the basilica to the home. Interestingly, the letter of 2 John speaks to this very problem. There we discover John warning a local assembly not to receive untested workers (2 John 10-11).

Regrettably, the second "house church movement" has been plagued by the opposite problem. It has failed to receive those whom God has genuinely sent. Interestingly enough, the message of 3 John addresses this very issue. John makes mention of Diotrephes who would not receive the traveling workers John sent to minister to the churches (3 John 1-11).

For our First Petition was that the reverend face of the Primitive and Apostolic Church should be brought back again to the eyes and knowledge of men.
-John Knox

CHAPTER 5

RESTORATION OR REVOLUTION?

In the latter part of the 20th century there has been a small surplus of books written on the restoration of the apostolic gift. Many of these books claimed that the 1990s would be "the decade of the apostle." They asserted with absolute certainly that God would raise up "thousands of apostles," restoring the apostolic ministry to the Body of Christ on a grand scale.

The 90s have passed us by and none of these high claims have come to pass. Nevertheless, some of these authors continue to carry on quite loudly about the "restoration" of the apostle and the other "five-fold ministry" gifts at some nebulous date in the future. You may not realize this, but this same "prediction" has been with us since 1948.[1] The literature, claims, exact rhetoric, and "prophecies" that were put to pen in that year are identical to what is being said today.

Some have called the "movement" that emphasizes the restoration of the ministry gifts—primarily the apostle and prophet—the *Restoration Movement*. This "movement" has been tried and found wanting. Instead, what is needed in the Body of Christ is not restoration. It is not even revival.[2] What is needed is *revolution*—a complete and radical change from

---

[1] While it has antecedents elsewhere during the 19th century, it picked up steam during the "Latter Rain Movement" in Canada in the late 1940s.

[2] Historically, revivals resurrect a dying church back to ground zero. Once the church is resurrected and the revival ends, the church continues on with the same unscriptural practices it had before it sunk into death. Revival, therefore, is merely a temporary solution to a long-term problem.

top to bottom. Revolution in our practice of the church. Revolution in our modern "Christian" mindset. And revolution in our ideas of church planting. Consider the following table that isolates the key differences between *Restoration* and *Revolution*:

Restoration	Revolution
"Apostles" are seen as wielding official authority over pastors and congregations. They typically engender fan-club followings, are treated like celebrities, and happily sport the title "apostle."	"Apostles" are largely hidden and broken vessels who sport no titles or offices. They usually work for a living. Most have a distaste for the word "apostle" and never use it to describe themselves.[3]
Emphasizes the victorious living of the individual Christian.	Emphasizes the corporate life and Christ-centered experience of the community of believers.
Emphasizes "spiritual gifts," "power," "signs and wonders."	Emphasizes the eternal purpose of God, the deeper work of the cross, and the centrality of Jesus Christ.
Measures success by large conferences and crusades that draw thousands.	Measures success by quality; ignores the size of the crowd.[4]
Stresses the spectacular things that God is "going to do" in the *future*.	Stresses the unsearchable riches that are available in Christ *now* and shows God's people how to appropriate them *today*.
Focuses on spiritual warfare and triumphing over the devil. (The devil gets almost as much air-play as the Lord does.)	Focuses on the glories of Jesus Christ. The devil is viewed as defeated and is largely ignored.

---

[3] The reason for this is because the term "apostle" has become corrupted, abused, and filled with an ego-inflated, unBiblical meaning.

[4] Throughout Paul's entire ministry, he only planted about 13 churches. Paul was more concerned with building *quality* than creating *quantity*.

Restoration	Revolution
Led by pastors, high-powered teachers, or all-powerful elders who do virtually all of the spoken ministry.	Led by *all* the brothers and sisters. They have been equipped to function and care for the church by extra-local workers who leave them on their own.
Singing is led by professional worship teams; the congregation simply follows the pre-arranged song selection.	Singing is led by *all* the brothers and sisters that make up the church.
Much talk about "equipping the saints" where they will be ready to minister in some elusive date in the future.	"Equipping the saints" is not a buzzword, but a reality. God's people minister *now* in the church meetings.
Sees the church as a fighting army, yet in reality it is an institution that requires a church building, a pastor, and a Sunday morning order of worship.	Sees the church as a free-flowing, beautiful woman—a new species, "the third race" that is inseparable from Jesus Christ Himself. The church building, the modern pastoral office, and the Sunday morning liturgy have been abandoned.
Embraces an old tiresome mindset that is rooted in Western individualism and 1800 years of ecclesiastical tradition.	Embraces an entirely new mindset that is rooted in the first-century story and the fellowship that exists in the Godhead.

As the Preacher of Ecclesiastes saw, "There is a time to break down, and a time to build up . . . a time to keep silence and a time to speak." And the second Reformation, if it comes, will be distinguished from the first by the fact that it is a time of reticence, of stripping down, of traveling light. The church will go through its baggage and discover how much it can better do without, alike in doctrine and in organization.
    -John A.T. Robinson

SECTION 2:

OBJECTIONS AND RESPONSES

Unfortunately, the subject of church planting is a highly charged issue for some Christians. The following section is a stab at preemptive peacemaking. But more so, it is written for those who have an open mind on the subject of church planting and who wish to cut through the fog that surrounds it.

CHAPTER 6

CAN THE NT EXAMPLE BE APPLIED TODAY?

Objection 1: Conditions are very different today in the Western World than they were in the first century. Back then the entire world was unsaved. There was no institutional church. Church planters like Paul did not take born-again Christians from institutional churches and teach them how to meet NT-style. Modern workers, therefore, cannot point to Paul as an example of what they do.

Granted, the apostolic mission of the first-century was one of pioneer evangelism into virgin territory. The gospel of Jesus Christ was brand new. There was no institutional church from which to draw (or rescue) Christians. Thus the bulk of Paul's converts fell into two categories: 1) Those who came straight from the pagan pool, and 2) God-fearing Gentiles who were institutionalized by the Jewish synagogues. Both were "virgin-soil" situations from a Christian standpoint.

But Paul's mission had two objectives. First, it was to convert lost souls. The second objective was interconnected with the first. It was to form local communities that bore corporate testimony to the kingdom of God.

Put another way, Paul's chief goal in preaching the gospel was to create Spirit-baptized communities that corporately express the Lord Jesus Christ. Eminent scholar D.J. Tidball echoes this thought saying,

Paul's primary interest was not in the conversion of individuals but in the formation of Christian communities.

("Social Setting of Mission Churches," Dictionary of Paul and His Letters)

Consider the following quotes that confirm this observation:

G.H. Lang:

An acute writer, contrasting the apostolic work with the more usual modern missionary methods has said that "we found missions, the apostles founded churches." The distinction is sound and pregnant. The apostles founded churches, and they founded nothing else, because for the ends in view nothing else was required or could have been so suitable. In each place where they laboured they formed converts into a local assembly . . . (The Churches of God)

Dave Norrington:

Paul relied on centrifugal evangelism (that is, going out and speaking the gospel to non-Christians), but he did so in order to establish Christian communities. (To Preach or Not to Preach?)

Stuart Murray:

The New Testament does not offer much support to evangelistic strategies that concentrate merely on the converting of individuals. (Church Planting: Laying Foundations)[1]

Roland Allen:

---

[1] The only exception in the entire NT that records a case of individual salvation is that of Philip leading the Ethiopian eunuch to the Lord (Acts 8:26ff.).

From what has already been said it is manifest that St. Paul did not go about as a missionary preacher merely to convert individuals: he went to establish churches from which the light might radiate throughout the whole country round. (Missionary Methods: St. Paul's or Ours?)

Howard Snyder:

The first task of every Christian is the edification of the community of believers. If we say that evangelism or soul winning is the first task of the believer, we do violence to the New Testament and place a burden on the backs of some believers that they are not able to bear. (The Community of the King)

Paul formed Christian communities by fathering, mothering, and nursing the Christians with which he worked (1 Thess. 2:7-12; 1 Cor. 4:15). He showed the church how to fellowship with its Lord, how to mature in Him corporately, how to function in its gatherings, and how to solve specific problems endemic to community life.

Tragically, these are things that most Christians in the institutional church know little about. To put it bluntly, being a seasoned Christian does not equip one to be a functioning member in a NT-styled church meeting. Nor does it prepare one to be a productive member of a Christian community. Neither does finding oneself 2000 years into Christian history and 500 years down the Reformation pike prepare one for such a task.

As A.W. Tozer once put it, the modern church "is an asylum for retarded spiritual children." It is a nursery for over-grown spiritual babes, most of whom do not have a clue about how to function with their fellow-brethren in a co-ordinated way. And why is this? Because they have never been shown how. Instead, they have been habituated to stay silent and passive. God's people, therefore, need to be unleashed and empowered.

The Pauline ministry of planting churches is still very much needed today. Far more goes into building a church than leading people to the Lord. Winning converts is merely a first step. Enriching, equipping, and empowering them to get on with God in a corporate way makes up the rest of the trip. Today, we have many living stones, but they are scattered and isolated. God's goal is for all of those stones to comprise a house. Therein lies the main calling of a worker (1 Cor. 3:9-10).

Consequently, if Paul were in the Western world today, it is extremely likely that he would seek out the lost sheep as well as the sheep who have strayed from the sheepfold. To be sure, Paul would present the gospel to lost souls. But hungry Christians in the institutional church would doubtlessly attach themselves to his work as well. Would Paul refuse to minister to them simply because they were "already" converted?

No, Paul's goal was a kingdom community. So he would undoubtedly minister to *all* of the saints who were open to him. Both new converts and institutionalized Christians. He would enrich them to know Christ, equip them to express Him corporately, and empower them to function in a co-ordinated way.

Genuine workers in our day do just that.

Not to put too fine a point on it, Paul's passion was to establish Christian communities (*churches*) marked by every-member functioning. It was not to rescue individuals from hell. We can be confident that if Paul were with us today, he would not be hindered from this all-consuming mission.

CHAPTER 7

WAS PAUL AN EXCEPTION?

Objection 2: The idea of a church being founded by or helped by a traveling worker is a theme found exclusively in Paul's ministry. The churches that weren't associated with Paul did not need outside help. In fact, some of these churches were founded without a worker. Therefore, you are overstating your case when you say that all churches today should have outside help.

Since Paul dominates the pages of the NT story, the principle of an extra-local worker founding and subsequently helping a church is most clearly seen in his ministry.

However, if you examine all the churches mentioned in the NT (there are over 30),[1] you will discover that every one of them was either founded by an itinerant worker or helped by one after its formation.

Paul and his company (e.g., Barnabas, Silas, Timothy, Titus, Epaphras, etc.) were not the only workers who traveled to plant, strengthen, and recenter churches. This was also true of the ministries of Peter, John, and (according to church

---

[1] According to the NT, there was a church planted in each of the following cities: Jerusalem, Damascus, Lydda, Joppa, Caesarea, Syrian Antioch, Salamis, New Paphos, Pisidian Antioch, Iconium, Lystra, Derbe, Troas, Philippi, Thessalonica, Berea, Corinth, Cenchrea, Ephesus, Laodicea, Colossae, Hierapolis, Smyrna, Thyatira, Sardis, Philadelphia, Pergamum, Tyre, Ptolemais, Rome, Nicopolis. If you add the churches mentioned in specific regions, the number increases. Again, all of these churches were either directly planted by or helped by an itinerant worker.

history) the rest of the Twelve. All of these men were "sent" to the "work" of building the church. Hence the reason why they are called "sent ones" (apostles) and "workers."

Some have argued that extra-local workers are an unnecessary artifact because several churches mentioned in the NT were not founded by one. People who employ this argument typically point to the churches that were formed during the Jerusalem dispersion. Let us explore again what really happened there.

The Jerusalem church was founded by the twelve apostles. They laid the foundation of that church for a period of *eight* years. After those eight years, the church in Jerusalem dispersed into Judea, Samaria, and Galilee. Some traveled to Cyprus. Others journeyed as far as Syria. The believers who dispersed into these new places began to meet just as they did in Jerusalem. And God added to their number as they shared the gospel with the lost.

As we have already seen in Chapter 1, the church in Jerusalem was *transplanted* into these other regions. In Acts 9:31 (NASB), Luke tells us that the church—singular—found rest in Judea, Galilee, and Samaria. In other words, the church in Jerusalem was relocated into these regions.

Keep in mind that the brethren who were part of these transplanted churches had: 1) Been initially helped by the twelve apostles for a period of eight years, and 2) Experienced the corporate life of the church in Jerusalem during those years.

In other words, the Jerusalem saints transplanted their *experience* of the church they received from the help of the apostles. They did not leave the synagogues one day and start house churches the next.

More importantly, after these newly transplanted churches were formed, they were subsequently helped by the apostles. The Jerusalem workers itinerantly circulated among the new churches (much like Paul's practice), ministering to them (Acts 8-12). This point is often overlooked.

Again, a careful study of the NT will yield that every church mentioned in the first-century story was either directly founded by or helped by extra-local workers. Thus the independent house church that rejects the help of itinerant workers shares one common feature with the institutional church. They both have no analog in the NT.

More pointedly, the itinerant worker giving birth to a church is a consistent pattern that runs throughout the NT. As we have seen, it is a principle that traces back to the Godhead before creation. For this reason, itinerant work is very much tied up with the fulfillment of God's eternal purpose. It is by no means an outdated practice.

CHAPTER 8

IS CHURCH PLANTING ELITIST?

Objection 3: The idea of an extra-local worker is an elitist notion. It elevates one person above everyone else. It creates a separate elitist class set apart to instruct "ordinary" believers. It is no different than the clergy that drives the institutional church. We Christians are the priesthood of God! All we need is Jesus! We do not need a man to help us! And we certainly do not need any "superstar" church planters to tell us what we already know! In fact, it is dangerous to have a church planter, because you are following a man and not God.

This objection sounds both noble and spiritual. But in reality, it is reactionary and misleading. The main problem with it is that it rejects a God-given ministry to the Body of Christ under the guise of "protecting" the priesthood of believers.

In philosophy, this is called a straw man argument. That is, it unfairly paints all workers as elitist men who set themselves above God's people. Then it effectively argues against this image by hiding behind the pious rhetoric of "just needing Jesus and not a man."

Indeed, there are false apostles who seek to fleece the sheep. There are untested and unsafe workers—control freaks if you will—who genuinely lord it over God's people.

But to castigate all who plant churches by a high-volume blow of inflammatory word-slinging (like "superstar," "elitist," "separate class," etc.) is to play upon people's pride and fear. Not to mention that it gives people a warped view of their fellow brethren in Christ.

The real kicker is that if we apply this objection to the NT story, the fallacy emerges in bold relief. Apply the logic of this objection and we would have to conclude the following: That Paul, Barnabas, Silas, Timothy, Titus, Epaphras and every other person who planted churches in the first century were "superstar" Christians who belonged to a "separate elitist class" set apart to instruct the poor "ordinary" believers!

We would have to also conclude that . . .

The churches in Galatia, Greece, and Asia Minor should have boldly told Paul, Barnabas, Silas, Timothy and Epaphras, "We do not need you. You are mere men. We do not need a man. We just need Jesus!"

If you buy into the mentality of "away with church planters, we just need Jesus," you are unwittingly saying, "Away with the Twelve, away with Paul, away with Barnabas, away with Silas, and away with Timothy!"

In addition, the idea that the church does not need a human being to assist it cannot be reconciled with the record of the early church. When Jesus Christ walked upon the earth in flesh and blood, one could rightly say, "We do not need anyone but Jesus."

But since He ascended and poured forth His Spirit, Jesus Christ has chosen to use men and women to accomplish His work on earth. The Lord Jesus uses people—flesh and blood—to preach the gospel, to plant and nurture churches. He uses people to instruct converts. He uses people to train and equip local fellowships.

No matter how you slice it, God has chosen to use man.

Hence, those who would push the "we do not need men, we only need Jesus" envelope fly in the face of NT revelation. It is specious thinking at its best.

To be sure, God's people need to be cautious of false apostles who seek to take advantage of them. But if we are serious about moving toward spiritual fullness, we will discerningly welcome the contributions of *all* whom God has placed in His Body. Including the role of the itinerant worker.

Itinerant workers, if they are the genuine article, are not spiritual elitists. They do not have a different status from other Christians. Instead, they are ordinary (and very imperfect) believers like everyone else. Only with a different calling.

They do not run local churches nor are they distant bosses over them. God is the only boss. Workers are simply highly valued servants to the churches they help. Their ties with the saints they work with are familial and relational. They are not official or hierarchical.

Some people in the Body of Christ have a gift for spotting and accessing the whole range of gifts and insights that a church is letting lie fallow. They have a talent for graciously redressing the church's weaknesses and keeping her from being distracted by those things that sap her energy. They also had a knack for getting the church to walk through those difficult mine fields that are necessary for making progress in the war of love.

They do not accomplish these things by pulpiteering or pontificating. Instead, they patiently and relentlessly minister, counsel, sit-and-talk, listen, coddle, encourage, empathize, and everything else they can think of to get people to look past the foibles of others and discover that they really can be brothers and sisters.

Such individuals are like catalysts in chemical reactions. They have a gift for galvanizing and catalyzing action among the rest of the Body. They inject fresh life into a church when its pulse begins to wane. They keep the foreign elements out so the church can grow up naturally and spontaneously. They recenter the saints when their eyes begin to move away from their only Center, Jesus Christ. Christian workers are those who are called to flesh out all of these things.

CHAPTER 9

CAN'T ANYONE START A HOUSE CHURCH?

Objection 4: Anyone can start a house church. You do not need to passively wait for a man to help you do this. I have had several children. I did not have any experience in raising kids before this. But I learned on the job. I did not need a man to help me give birth to my babies or raise them. Therefore, I do not need a man to show me how to start a house church. I can just start one. And so can anyone else.

This objection really misses the point about what Scripture teaches about church planting. Anyone, even a baby Christian, can start a home group. All it takes is a willingness to open your home and allow your fellow Christians to sit in comfy couches in your living room. Add a little Java to the mix with a weekly Bible study, and presto, you have founded your own "house church."

But does this brand of church have any points of contact with the churches that we read about in our NTs?[1] Does this sort of a gathering reach any further toward fulfilling God's eternal purpose than does the institutional church . . . or a slice-and-dice cell church . . . or a 12-step recovery group?

If this is the extent of your vision of the church, then itinerant workers are unnecessary.

---

[1] Some have used Matthew 18:20 as a proof text to support the idea that if two or three Christians gather together in a home, they are a church. But this passage is not defining the critical mass for a church. It is instead referring to an excommunication meeting (see Matt. 18:15ff.).

But if you have been captured by a vision of the church where every member contributes something of Christ to the gatherings. A vision where Christ is continually being experienced, made visible, central, and supreme. A vision where principalities and powers are shamed by the church's testimony. Then you do well to remember Paul's words: *"But God has set some in the church, first apostles, secondarily prophets, thirdly teachers . . . Are all apostles? are all prophets? are all teachers?" (1 Cor. 12:28-29).*

For Paul, the unmistakable answer is "no." God has gifted His people with different gifts and functions. And that includes those who are "sent" to plant and nurture churches from the outside.

Therefore, the logic that says "since I can give birth to babies, then I can give birth to a first-century styled church" is invalid. God has "set" some in the Body for this task, just as He has set others in the Body for other tasks.

People can escape into theories all day about the help or hindrance of extra-local workers. But the issue really boils down to the kind of church life you are seeking to have.

Most modern house churches that have never been "outside helped" function in one of the following ways:

Profile 1. Every week one person will give a Bible lesson or teaching. The rest of the church passively listens. There may be some dialogue about what the teacher taught. There may even be questions offered during the lesson. But the meeting is centered around a sermon-like oration. Some churches have rotating elders that teach the church to passivity. Others are open to have others teach. But this way of meeting is essentially a glorified Bible study or a teaching station.

Profile 2. Often a sub-set of the first group, some house churches are so doctrinaire that their meetings often degenerate into endless doctrinal debates about endless precise formulations of an endless variety of endless theological minutiae. In short, their gatherings do nothing more than swell the cranium and raise the blood pressure.

Profile 3. Meetings are marked by heaps of passivity. Most are quiet and never say a word. The silence is sometimes deafening. When someone does speak, it is typically a general sharing about someone's personal struggles. Or it may be some interesting idea that a person had during the week. Perhaps verses from the Bible are aimlessly read. There is little direction, harmony, or life in the meeting. Jesus Christ is not the driving content. Nor can it be rightly said that He is manifesting Himself in the meeting.

Profile 4. The meeting is a songfest. There is a music leader that leads the singing. It may be a guitar player who "leads worship." Having all the saints lead their own singing, even to the writing of their own songs, is never seen.

Profile 5. There is little to no interaction between members outside of the weekly meetings. The house church is "meeting-oriented." It is not a community of shared, integrated lives. Biblically speaking, this is an abnormal situation. Consider the words of R. Paul Stevens,

> *. . . There is no such thing as an individual member . . . "the individual Christian" is an oxymoron. Consistent with the Old Testament, the "saints" in Paul's letters is really a unit. As Ernest Best says, "it is this unit which is just as much in Christ as the individual believer." Believers are held together in what can be conceived as a corporate, inclusive per-*

sonality. It is biblically and theologically inconceivable for a person to be a believer in Christ and not a member of His community. So for Paul "there is no such thing as a solitary Christian" and "it is impossible to conceive of a Christian who is not a member of the church, which is related to Christ as in Him and as His Body . . . Individual Christians consequently do not exist." (The Abolition of the Laity)

Profile 6. Human relationships are deified and stand as the substitute for a living, corporate relationship to the Head of the church. There is no understanding of God's eternal purpose. The church has little to no experience in handling Christ spiritually. It knows little about receiving from Him and manifesting Him in a gathering whereby visitors say, "I have seen the Lord like I have never seen Him before!"

Granted, there are house churches that have never received help from an experienced worker that do not map to any of these ways. If you belong to one, then you are the rare exception.

Some people get aggressively antagonistic when the subject of church planting comes up. The emotionally laden and highly flammable reactions to the mere mention of it suggests that a nerve is being probed somewhere. It is nearly impossible to sort through the melange of motivations that lay behind these reactions. But let us unearth the more common ones.

For some, the sore spot is the result of a bad experience with a worker that has left them bitter and reactionary. So now they lump all workers into the same contaminated camp. To use Lessing's unfortunate phrase, untrustable workers, just like modern pastors, are the "accidental truths of history." And historical accidents ought never to be taken as the norm by which to judge all spiritual leadership.

Another reason for the backlash against outside help has its roots in certain abuses that took place during the Jesus movement. Some have responded to these abuses by championing the cause of "anti-leadership."

Regrettably, many of God's people have suffered under authoritarian leadership models. Yet those who have moved to the opposite extreme and wave the "anti-leadership" flag perpetuate their own brand of oppression.

"Anti-leadership" has the net effect of gutting all leadership language out of the NT. It deludes itself into believing that by "taking a stand" against leaders we have accomplished something righteous and noble.

Some "anti-leaders" are active and bellicose, chafing against all those who have an influence in the lives of God's people. Others are passive aggressives who have the remarkable ability to stalemate any church by insisting that no one ever lead anything.

This typically results in a church "led" manipulatively and subversively by the person that refuses to let others lead. And by and large, the "second state is worse than the first."

On the darker side, there is something lurking within some men's hearts that objects to receiving help from others. Such individuals mask the real reason for their opposition by vilifying those who plant churches. (If you listen to their half-clear ravings carefully enough, the real motive will eventually slip out of their mouths.)

There is a gentleman mentioned in the NT who refused to receive workers whom John the apostle sent to strengthen the churches (3 John 5-11). John laid bare the dark motive that lay behind the rejection of God-sent workers. It was because this man "loved to have the preeminence" in the church!

This man very well may have concealed his desire for prominence by hiding behind the "we do not need these workers, we just need Jesus" platitude. But underneath these words he was really saying, "I do not want anyone to follow the ministry of *another* man. I am afraid of losing *my* place of influence and prominence in the eyes of the church. I want the saints to look to *me* instead of someone else." Those who claim that the church does not need any kind of leadership are those who wish to be leaders themselves.

The irony here is that one of the roles of an extra-local worker is to protect the church from those local brethren suffering from *apostle-itis,* clamoring for the attention of God's people.

In his book, *Lost in the Cosmos,* Walker Percy summarizes the human problem by pressing the following questions: Are you in trouble? If you are, have you sought help? If help came, did you accept it?

Percy makes the penetrating observation that many modern folk are in trouble but do not know it. They have never bothered to seek help. And they would not accept it if it came. This point warrants sober reflection. We who have left the institutional church are ripe to seek the Lord in humility about this issue. It is high time we swallow our initial re-actions and confront and subdue our bitterness, prejudice, and theories, asking God to give us His light—and if necessary, His healing.

In a nutshell, a worker's task is to work himself out of a job. After he spends considerable time planting the church, his time with that church should always be a temporary affair. It comes in spurts. And he is absent more than he is present.

Initially, his influence and the time he spends laying a foundation for a church will be intense. But after the foun-dational phase is finished, he will leave the church on its own. This does not mean that he will not keep in contact with the church at all. For what good parent does not keep in contact with his children after they leave home—especially if they get into trouble? As Roland Allen states,

St. Paul was careful not to lose touch with his converts. They sorely needed visits and instruction, and they received them. I have no doubt that he was in constant communication with them by one means or another. But there is an immense difference between dealing with an organized church through letters and messengers and occasional visits, and exercising direct personal government . . . Nothing can alter or disguise the fact that he succeeded in so training his converts that men who came to him absolutely ignorant of the gospel were able to maintain their position with the help of occasional letters and visits at crises of special difficulty. (Missionary Methods: St. Paul's or Ours?)

While the church is on its own after the worker lays its foundation, he will return periodically to strengthen, recenter, and build on the foundation he has laid. He may also return if there is a crisis.

Depending on its spiritual pulse, sometimes the church will call for intense involvement from the worker; other times the involvement will be minimal. Paul is an example for us here. His involvement in Corinth was far more intense and ongoing than his involvement in Berea. It all had to do with the condition of the church and its present needs.

All that to say: If a worker is doing his job properly, his involvement in the church's affairs over the long haul will be fairly minimal. This prevents the worker from laming God's people.

The worker's ministry thrives in a spiritual culture that appreciates leadership without deifying it. The modern worker, like Paul, plays a visible role in the birth and ongoing life of the churches he founds. You can find that in Robert Banks if you are looking for a footnote.[2]

---

[2] *Dictionary of Paul and His Letters* (Downers Grove: InterVarsity Press, 1993), p. 136.

CHAPTER 10

ARE CHURCH PLANTERS REALLY NECESSARY?

Objection 6: If a church wants outside help, they can get it from discussion lists, by having members of other house churches visit them, and by visiting other house churches themselves. Why settle for an extra-local worker when you can avail yourself of a bunch of help from many different sources? Related to this, failures and problems are taking place in house churches under the leadership of itinerant workers just as much as they are in house churches that do not have the aid of a Christian worker.

This objection is built on faulty logic. The question of getting outside help from a worker vs. other churches is not an either/or issue. To pit it this way grossly confuses the matter and ends up producing balkanized, warring camps. Certainly, outside help is not relegated to the ministry of an itinerant worker. Churches can and should receive help and encouragement from other churches and from gifted individuals within those churches. This was the practice of the first-century church.

On one critical occasion, the church in Antioch, Syria helped the church in Jerusalem (Acts 11:29). The church in Jerusalem sometimes sent some of her prophets and teachers to Antioch to help strengthen and instruct the church there (Acts 11:27; 15:22).

Interrelatedness and interdependence among the early churches was critical.[1] But it never replaced the twelve apostles' unique relationship with Jerusalem. Nor did it replace Paul and Barnabas' unique relationship with Antioch. David Shenk and Ervin Stutzman bring out a related point about the interrelatedness among the early churches saying,

> *Nevertheless, planting isolated churches was not the intent of their mission. The congregations of Asia Minor clustered in a general region and the church planters returned to visit each of the new fellowships in order to give them encouragement. Certainly a significant aspect of that encouragement was to report what God had done in other cities. They shared the good news that sister congregations had been planted in adjoining communities. (Creating Communities of the Kingdom)*

While networking among local churches is important, it can never replace that special fatherly relationship that exists between a worker and the church he has established. The relationship that Paul of Tarsus had with the churches he planted is a case in point. It could not be displaced.

Nothing—especially the stale medium of a computer discussion list—can replace the personal time that an experienced worker spends with a group of Christians. There is no substitute for the spiritual dynamic that occurs when such a person ministers Christ face-to-face with a group of believers—showing them how to experience Him in practical ways, giving them concrete help in expressing Him cor-

---

[1] The churches of the first century often helped one another (Acts 14:21-28; 15:3-4; 21:17-19; Rom. 15:25-27; 2 Cor. 8:14-24). Those who plant churches should encourage such interrelatedness among the churches with which they work.

porately, and helping them find Him in the midst of a problem. Remember, God has sovereignly set such people in the Body (1 Cor. 12:28; Eph. 4:11-16). As Paul said, "The eye cannot say to the hand, I have no need of you" (1 Cor. 12:21).

At bottom, the suggestion that workers can be easily replaced by discussion lists and inter-church relationships is in disharmony with the spirit and practice of NT Christianity. It also reveals a lack of understanding as to what a worker actually does when he serves a church.

To come the long way round to the question: Should a house church be benefited by itinerant workers or should it be benefited by other means? The answer is that we do not have to land in one of these two hopelessly polarized camps. Why not avail ourselves of all helpful resources? It is not an either/or situation.

Do church planters fail at what they do? Yes. Church planters are just as frail and mortal as everyone else. They have the same foibles, eccentricities, and weaknesses as do other believers—sometimes worse.

What is more, every house church will face problems and experience failures. It matters not if they were founded or helped by an itinerant worker.

Consider that virtually all the churches that Paul planted had problems. (We are never told about the problems in the churches of Berea, Troas, or Cenchrea. But given the volatile nature of church life, we can safely assume that they had their share of woes.)

Consequently, the presence of an itinerant worker will never prevent a church from undergoing problems and failures. Often, the difference is in *how* those problems and failures are handled when they arrive. A house church that has no outside resource is totally on its own when it faces a crisis. It is like the proverbial boat that is stuck in the raging sea without oars. Self-correction can only go so far. This is because in virtually every case those within the group are in some way part of the problem!

When outside help is present, the church possesses an external resource that knows the church well on the one hand, but is not part of the problem on the other. These two features, coupled with his spiritual and practical experience, makes the worker an invaluable benefit to a church that is undergoing difficulty.

Many years of wandering around the wilderness might be spared if there is an experienced person from the outside who can give the church guidance, encouragement, and direction. Such guidance should always be given with a view to equipping the church so that she can eventually build *herself* up. Granted, an itinerant worker is not a panacea. But he is a resource that can help a church tremendously.

CHAPTER 11

WASN'T PAUL THE LAST CHURCH PLANTER?

Objection 7: Didn't Paul say that he was the last apostle? And didn't he say that one of the evidences of an apostle is to see Jesus Christ? Therefore, apostles (church planters) have passed away, haven't they?

First, Paul never said that he was the last apostle. And there is no Scripture in the NT that states that the ministry of the apostle has passed away.

In 1 Corinthians 15:8-9, Paul said that he was the *least* apostle, not the *last*. He also said that he was the last person to see Jesus Christ physically after about 500 others saw Him. But Paul never stated that he was the last person to see the Risen Lord. Such assertions must be read into the text. They cannot be found in Paul's actual words.

In two of Paul's last letters, he states that God has set in the Body of Christ "sent ones," that is, apostles (1 Cor. 12:28; Eph. 4:11). There is no Scripture anywhere that overturns, nullifies, or cancels out these statements. To do so is to speak where Scripture has not spoken.

If that is not enough, the last book of the NT, which was penned after Paul's death, records the words of Jesus regarding the testing of false apostles.[1] If a church must test whether or not a person is a true apostle, this by necessity

---

[1] The mark of a false apostle is one of the following: He seeks money, fame, or supplants the work of other men.

means that true apostles exist (Rev. 2:2). C. Peter Wagner writes,

Curiously, until fairly recently, I did not notice what now appears to me to be an inconsistency in what I had been taught: Our ideal was that the church be led by the apostles, but supposedly no apostles were to be found in our churches today! Having accepted such a premise, it would then become clear that we would replicate the first-century church today only if apostles were a trivial or relatively insignificant component of first-century Christianity. No biblical scholar I know, however, would affirm that. Apostles were a recognized key to the vitality of the early church . . . I now believe we can begin to approach the spiritual vitality and power of the first-century church only if we recognize, accept, receive and minister in all the spiritual gifts, including the gift of apostle. ("Foreword" in Apostles and the Emerging Apostolic Movement)

Speaking in the same spirit, Howard Snyder says,

Because of the obvious uniqueness of the original apostles, some have argued that apostles no longer exist today. But this conclusion runs counter to the Biblical evidence and makes too sharp a break between the original apostles and the church leaders who followed them . . . It cannot be successfully maintained, therefore, that the apostolic ministry passed away with the death of the original Twelve . . . Scripture teaches that the Spirit continually and charismatically gives to the church the function of apostle. (The Community of the King)

In another place, Wagner argues:

. . . Ephesians goes on to say that we still need apostles and prophets. It says that when Jesus ascended into heaven,

"[He] gave gifts to men" (Eph. 4:8). What were these gifts? "He Himself gave some to be apostles, some prophets, some evangelists, and some pastors and teachers" (Eph. 4:11). Generally speaking, we have been comfortable with evangelists, pastors, and teachers in our churches. But some have had a serious problem with apostles and prophets. There is, however, little justification for drawing an imaginary exegetical line between the first two offices and the latter three in the same verse. Apostles and prophets belong there, but for how long? "Till we all come to the unity of the faith and the knowledge of the Son of God, to a perfect man, to the measure of the stature of the fullness of Christ" (Eph. 4:12). I don't know anyone who would say that the church as we know it has reached this stage of unity and perfection. Therefore, it seems, we still need apostles and prophets. (Apostles of the City)

What follows is a list of all the apostles mentioned in the NT:

Jesus Christ (Heb. 3:1)

The Twelve (Matt. 10:2-4, Mark 3:14-19, Luke 6:13-16):[2]

- Andrew
- Bartholomew (also called Nathanael)
- James, son of Zebedee
- James, son of Alphaeus
- John
- Judas Iscariot (Matthias took his place—Acts 1:26)
- Judas (also called Lebbaeus and surnamed Thaddaeus)
- Matthew (also called Levi)
- Peter (also called Simon)

---

[2] The Twelve have special prominence that is not shared with any other apostle who followed them (Matt. 19:28; Rev. 21:14).

- Philip
- Simon Zelotes (also called Simon the Canaanite)
- Thomas (also called Didymus)

In addition to the Twelve, the following are also called "apostles" (*apostolos* in the Greek):

- Apollos (1 Cor. 4:6-9)
- Andronicus (Rom. 16:7)
- Barnabas (Acts 14:3-4, 14; 1 Cor. 9:5-6)
- Epaphroditus (Phil. 2:25)
- James the Lord's brother (1 Cor. 15:7; Gal. 1:19)
- Junias (Rom. 16:7)[3]
- Paul (Gal. 1:1; Eph. 1:1; Col. 1:1, et al.)
- Silas (1 Thess. 1:1; 2:6)
- Timothy (1 Thess. 1:1; 2:6)
- Titus (2 Cor. 8:23)

Clearly, the NT makes evident that Paul was not the last apostle and that apostles still exist in the church today.

Second, the idea that an apostle must physically see Jesus has no support from the NT either. Some have pointed to 1 Cor. 9:1 where Paul asks, *"Have I not seen Jesus Christ our Lord?,"* to prove that apostles must see the Risen Lord. But

---

[3] Junia is most likely a woman apostle. For that is how the early church fathers interpreted this passage. In fact, no commentator until the 13th century took the name as masculine (See Robert Banks, *Paul's Idea of Community*, Hendrickson, p. 155; Charles Trombley, *Who Said Women Can't Teach?*, South Plainfield: Bridge Publishing, 1985, pp. 190-191). See also F.F. Bruce, *The Pauline Circle* (Grand Rapids: Eerdmans, 1985), p. 83. Bruce writes of Andronicus and Junia, "Jewish believers whose faith in Christ antedated Paul's. 'They are of note among the apostles,' Paul adds (Rom. 16:7), meaning that they were not only known to the apostles but eminent apostles themselves . . ."

Paul was not stating that an apostle must see Christ. He made that statement along with another: *"Am I not free?"* Freedom is not a qualification for being an apostle, for Paul was not free for at least four years of his life. Was he not an apostle during these years of Roman imprisonment?

If you continue to read the passage, Paul argues that his apostleship is evidenced by the fruits of his labors—*"are you not my work in the Lord?"* rather than his being free or having seen the Lord Jesus. While it is true that all twelve apostles saw the Resurrected Christ physically (including Matthias), this is not true for many of the other apostles that came after the Twelve. Nevertheless, what is true for all Christian workers is that each of them has a deep and living revelation of Jesus Christ. For upon such revelation the church is built (Matt. 16:16-18; 1 Cor. 3:11).

Some have charged men who have a unique revelation of Christ as being "mystical." There is no doubt that Paul had such a revelation. Men and women who follow in his footsteps should own such a revelation also. Whether one calls it "mystical" or "spiritual" is irrelevant. The point is that they are in need of "knowing" the Lord in reality if they will lead others to know Him in reality (Gal. 1:16; 1 Cor. 2:7ff.; Php. 3:10). Remarking on Paul of Tarsus' mystical side, F. F. Bruce writes,

According to Albert Schweitzer, Paul's mysticism is unique because, in spite of its high intellectual level, it does not take the form of direct union with God but rather of union with Christ. "In Paul," he says, "there is no God-mysticism; only a Christ-mysticism by means of which man comes into relation to God . . . This "being-in-Christ" is the prime enigma of the Pauline teaching: once grasped it gives the clue to the whole" . . . such phrases as "in Christ Jesus" (quoted above) or "in Christ" or "in the Lord" are characteristic of Paul, and it is the concept which they express that is often in view (as with Schweitzer) when people speak of "Pauline mysticism" . . . Perhaps R.C. Tannehill has the answer. Defining mysticism as "the doctrine that the individual can come into immediate contact with God through subjective experiences which differ essentially from the experiences of daily life," he adds: "By this definition Paul may be spoken of as, among other things, a 'mystic' (cf. his visions, 2 Cor. 12:1-4), but he does not have a mystical theology." This last point is well taken: Paul's theology was not based on experiences which might be described as mystical: it is based on Jesus, the fulfiller of God's promise and purpose of salvation; Jesus, the crucified and exalted Lord; Jesus, the Divine wisdom, in whom God creates, maintains and brings to consummation everything that exists: Jesus, who here and now lives within His people by His Spirit. (Paul: Apostle of the Heart Set Free)

CHAPTER 12

DON'T CHURCH PLANTERS PERFORM SIGNS AND WONDERS?

Objection 8: Didn't Paul say that signs and wonders are the marks of a true apostle? Therefore, if someone claims to be a church planter but does not perform signs and wonders, doesn't this mean that he is not a true apostle?

The idea that signs and wonders mark an apostle's ministry has been misunderstood and misapplied since the turn of the 20th century. According to Paul, the principal evidence of apostleship is the founding of a church (1 Cor. 9:1; 2 Cor. 3:1-3; 13:3-6).

In 2 Corinthians 12:12, Paul lists other evidences of a worker. He writes,

> *The things which are the characteristic hall-marks of any apostle happened among you. You saw me live a life in which again and again I passed the breaking-point and did not break, a life marked by demonstrations of the power of God in action, by wonders and miracles.*

According to this passage, the signs of a church planter can be distilled down to two elements: Spiritual power and miraculous power. At the top of Paul's list of qualifications is the hallmark of spiritual power: Perseverance. The Greek word translated "passed the breaking-point and did not break," or "perseverance" and "patience" in other translations, is *hupomone*. It means to abide under pressure. It is "the characteristic of a man who is not swerved from his deliberate purpose and his loyalty to faith and piety by even the greatest trials and sufferings."[1] Watchman Nee put it beautifully when he said,

> *. . . the signs of an apostle will never be lacking where there is truly an apostolic call . . . Endurance is the greatest proof of spiritual power, and it is one of the signs of an apostle. It is the ability to endure steadfastly under the continuous pressure that tests the reality of an apostolic call. (The Normal Christian Church Life)*

Paul's words to the Ephesian elders capture his relentless ambition to endure to the end and finish the race that God called him to run. His words are an insight into his incredible perseverance:

> *. . . the Holy Spirit testifies in every city, saying that bonds and afflictions await me. But none of these things move me, neither do I count my life dear to myself, so that I might finish my course with joy, and the ministry, which I have received of the Lord Jesus . . . (Acts 20:23-24)[2]*

Miraculous power is another sign of a church planter. Miraculous power is God's ability to change situations in the physical realm. First-century workers accessed God's power in the face of impending situations that challenged the Lord and His name. He would pray for the sick at times. And he would effect the Holy Spirit's power in high pressure situations.

But miraculous power is all-too often misunderstood. Surprisingly, out of all the apostles mentioned in the NT, only

---

[1] Strong's Exhaustive Concordance.
[2] See also Paul's catalog of sufferings that he endured in 2 Corinthians 11.

three are recorded as performing signs and wonders: Jesus, Peter, and Paul.[3]

In Paul's ministry alone, miracles are recorded in only *eight* towns: Paphos, Iconium, Lystra, Philippi, Corinth, Ephesus, Troas, and Malta.[4] It is an invalid assumption, therefore, to conclude that Paul performed miracles everywhere he went. As Roland Allen explains,

> *Thus it would appear that the importance of miracles in the work of St. Paul may be easily exaggerated. They were not a necessary part of his mission preaching: nor was their influence in attracting converts as great as we often suppose . . . their [miracles] importance can be easily overrated and it is manifest that St. Paul saw this danger and combated it. He does not give the gift of miracles the highest place amongst the gifts of the Spirit. He does not speak as if the best of his workers possessed it. It was not the power of working miracles which was of importance in his eyes: it was the Spirit which inspired the life. (Missionary Methods: St. Paul's or Ours?)*

So the miraculous will be present in the ministry of the modern church planter, but only at those times when it is necessary according to the mind of God.

---

[3] Barnabas is said to have performed miracles along *with* Paul (Acts 14:3; 15:12). There are only two non-apostles that are recorded as performing signs and wonders: Stephen (Acts 6:8) and Philip (Acts 8:6). Acts 2:43 and 5:12 are the only places where "the apostles" (plural) are said to have performed signs and wonders.

[4] Acts 13:6-12; 14:3, 8-10; 16:18; 19:11-12; 20:9-12; 28:3-9; 2 Cor. 12:12.

CHAPTER 13

THE NEED OF THE HOUR

The Divine principle of extra-local, itinerant work is the forgotten chapter in the first-century story. It is the overlooked pattern of the early church. It is the neglected ministry in the Body of Christ. And yet there is far more Biblical currency for this pattern than there is for home meetings, plural elders, open-participatory gatherings, and every other practice that those who meet in homes arduously defend with chapter and verse.

If we will see a richer and higher expression of the Body of Christ, it is ours to return to the first principles of God's work. If we do not, God's timeless purpose will suffer loss. Doubtlessly, we will continue to see many small bands of Christians leaving the organized church, assembling in homes, sitting on comfy couches, and conversing over Java and cookies.

But this is a far cry from that majestic, unfathomable, high and mighty eternal purpose that God has called His people to work out. Namely, that they would make Jesus Christ in all of His fullness visible on this planet. And that His people would become experientially one with Him—the mystery of all mysteries!

Nothing less than a revolution of primitive Christian thinking and church practice will fulfill God's eternal purpose. In order to foment such a revolution, what is needed are men who are called by God to raise up the Lord's house. Broken and tested men. Men who have *first* lived in Body life as brothers before they dare start a church. Men who have a deep and living relationship with Jesus Christ. Men who have profound insight into the mystery of God. Men whose only passion is the Lord and His house. Men who have a revelation of Christ that burns in their being. And men who have the ability to preach only Him until God's people are left staggering.

The need of the hour is for such men to wait on God until they are trained and sent. And once sent, to plant the church in the same way that all first-century workers did—by equipping it and then abandoning it to the Holy Spirit!

Equally needed is for the Body of Christ to recognize the role of such men. May the scores of modern Christians who are leaving institutional Christianity see their need for itinerant workers and cease from blithely ignoring their God-given stewardship (1 Cor. 12:18-21,28; Eph. 4:7-16).

Today is a day of repairing and mending. And repairing the corporate testimony of God's people is no small thing. While there is no shortage of Christians in the West, there is a great dearth in the way of corporate testimony. God's foremost desire is to secure a people in every locale that are foundationally constituted and built together as a visible, locatable, geographical, corporate expression of His Son (Col. 2:2,19; Eph. 2:21-22; 4:16; 1 Pet. 2:5).

Christians who have left the institutional church, no matter how long they have been saved, will have an awfully hard time going on with other Christians in a face-to-face community without human headship. Thus workers who know the Headship of Christ—who have experienced genuine church life with all of its glory and gore—and who have been broken by the cross—are an indispensable resource for helping believers discover how to gather under Christ's direct Headship today.

Dear Christian who is seeking to gather in first-century fashion—if you will firmly hold to the NT pattern of how the early church met, how can you reject the NT pattern of how the church is planted? If you feel obligated to embrace NT principle on matters of church order, are you not equally obligated to embrace NT principle on the matter of church planting? And if you feel called to plant churches, are you not obligated to pay heed to God's way of preparing men for this work?

BIBLIOGRAPHY

The following bibliography includes the principal publications quoted in this book along with others that are germane to the topic.

Allen, Roland. *Missionary Methods: St. Paul's or Ours?*, Eerdmans. Classic work setting forth Paul's strategy of planting indigenous churches that are self-governing, self-propagating, and self-supporting.

_____. *The Spontaneous Expansion of the Church*, World Dominion Press. The sequel to the above book, this volume examines how the church organically and naturally expands and identifies the causes that hinder this expansion.

Austin-Sparks, T. *Captivity in the Lord*, Emmanuel Church. Insightful little booklet expounding the Lord's way of making His servants fit for use.

_____. *Leadership and Ministry*, Three Brothers. Deeply spiritual look at leadership and ministry in the Lord's work.

_____. *Prophetic Ministry*, Testimony Book Ministry. Classic treatment on what it means to minister Jesus Christ prophetically.

_____. *The More Excellent Ministry*, Testimony Book Ministry. Profound look at what it means to be a steward of the mystery of God.

_____. *The Spiritual Meaning of Service*, Testimony Book Ministry. Illuminating discussion on the principles of Divine service from God's standpoint.

_____. *The Stewardship of the Mystery: Volumes I & II*, Testimony Book Ministry. An extraordinary, breath-taking vision of the purpose of the ages, which is the basis for all church planting.

Banks, Robert. *Paul's Idea of Community*, Hendrickson. The last chapters contain an excellent discussion on Paul's non-authoritarianism when it came to planting and nurturing churches.

Bruce, A.B. *The Training of the Twelve*, Kregel. Classic and comprehensive work describing Jesus' method of training the apostles.

Bruce, F.F. *Paul, Apostle of the Heart Set Free*, Eerdmans. The best book in print discussing Paul's life, theology, and mission.

_____. *The Book of the Acts (Revised): New International Commentary on the New Testament*, Eerdmans. Regarded by many as the best scholarly commentary on the book of Acts available.

_____. *The Pauline Circle*, Eerdmans. Informative survey on Paul's friends, assistants, and co-workers.

Coleman, Robert. *The Master Plan of Evangelism*, Revell. Popular volume explaining how Jesus trained the twelve apostles.

Conybeare, W.J. and J.S. Howson. *The Life and Epistles of St. Paul*, Eerdmans. Voluminous treatment of Paul's journeys in chronological order. While some of the scholarship is outdated, it remains a classic treatment of Paul's church planting trips.

Edwards, Gene. *Climb the Highest Mountain,* Seedsowers. Insightful discussion on the problems that house churches face today and how workers should conduct themselves in the face of them.

_____. *First-Century Diaries,* Tyndale House. A series of five books that tell the story of Paul's church planting trips in novel form.

_____. *How to Meet in Homes,* Seedsowers. One of the best books written on how Paul planted churches and the need to restore this work today.

_____. *Overlooked Christianity,* Seedsowers. Excellent discussion on how Jesus and Paul trained workers.

_____. *The Americanization of Christianity,* Seedsowers. A prophetic plea against modern missionary methods.

_____. *The Early Church,* Christian Books. Excellent narrative on the first seventeen years of the early church. The 1974 edition contains a very insightful appendix that lists 22 qualifications of a modern apostle.

Fromke, Devern. *The Ultimate Intention,* Sure Foundation. Classic treatment systematically unfolding God's eternal purpose.

Grenz, Stanley. *Theology for the Community of God,* Broadman & Holman Publishers. Fantastic systematic theology that discusses all of theology from the vantage point of God as Community and His intention to establish community in creation.

Hodges, Melvin. *A Guide to Church Planting,* Moody Press. While written from an institutional paradigm, this is a solid discussion on some of the more basic principles of church planting.

Latham, Henry. *Pastor Pastorum or The Schooling of the Apostles by our Lord,* Deighton Bell & Co. Lengthy discussion on some of the lessons that Jesus taught the Twelve by precept and example.

Murray, Stuart. *Church Planting: Laying Foundations,* Herald Press. Scholarly discussion on the subject of church planting.

Nee, Watchman. *Church Affairs,* Christian Fellowship Publishers. Superb look at the first-century methods of church planting. Its weakness is that it gives "official" authority to elders.

_____. *Spiritual Knowledge,* Christian Fellowship Publishers. Incisive discussion on the various aspects of receiving spiritual light from God.

_____. *The Normal Christian Church Life,* Living Stream Ministry. Probably the best work ever written explaining the Antioch model of church planting.

_____. *The Character of God's Workman,* Christian Fellowship Publishers. Great discussion on the principle characteristics of a Christian worker.

_____. *The Ministry of God's Word,* Christian Fellowship Publishers. Indepth treatment on what it means to minister Christ to people.

_____. *The Release of the Spirit,* Sure Foundation. Insightful look at the means God uses to break those He calls to His service.

Pinnock, Clark. *Flame of Love: A Theology of the Holy Spirit*, InterVarsity Press. Excellent treatment on the Holy Spirit's role in the Divine Community between Father and Son and His role in creating the church as the community that emerges out of the Godhead.

Robinson, John A.T. *The New Reformation?*, The Westminster Press. Ahead of its time, this work looks at how God is seeking to restore His church to its proper form.

Rumble, Donald. *Apostolic & Prophetic Foundations,* The Attic Studio Press. Solid discussion on various principles of apostolic ministry.

Shenk, David and Ervin Stutzman. *Creating Communities of the Kingdom,* Herald Press. Great discussion on Paul's method of planting churches with special emphasis on the kingdom of God.

Snyder, Howard. *The Community of the King,* InterVarsity Press. Superb discussion on the church as the community of the kingdom of God.

Stevens, R. Paul. *The Abolition of the Laity,* Paternoster Press. Superb look at the peril of clericalism from many different vantage points. Special emphasis on the kingdom of God and a theology of every day life.

Viola, Frank. *Pagan Christianity,* Present Testimony Ministry. Traces the unbiblical origins of our modern church practices.

_____. *Rethinking the Wineskin*, Present Testimony Ministry. Compares and contrasts the modern church with the first-century church.

_____. *Straight Talk to Elders*, Present Testimony Ministry. A thorough and compelling look at how elders functioned in the early church.

_____. *Who is Your Covering?*, Present Testimony Ministry. Compares and contrasts first-century leadership with the modern practice of leadership. Discusses Paul's idea of authority and contrasts it with the practice of modern leaders and self-appointed "apostles."

OTHER BOOKS IN THIS SERIES

Volume 1: Rethinking the Wineskin: The Practice of the New Testament Church. This is Frank Viola's classic book on the first-century church. It demonstrates beyond dispute that the modern institutional church has no Scriptural right to exist!

Volume 2: Who is Your Covering? A Fresh Look at Leadership, Authority, and Accountability. This book explores the issues of church leadership and spiritual authority in much more depth than *Wineskin.*

Volume 3: Pagan Christianity: The Origins of Our Modern Church Practices. A unique work that traces every modern Protestant practice, proving that it has no root in the NT.

Volume 5: From Nazareth to Patmos: The Saga of the New Testament Church. A synopsis of the entire story of the first-century church in its chronological, historical, and social context.

Straight Talk to Elders. This book could have just as easily been titled *Straight Talk to Pastors.* A thorough survey from Matthew to Revelation on the role and function of first-century elders (pastors).

Knowing Christ Together. An insightful book that explores the subject of knowing and walking with the Lord with other believers.

The Untold Story of the New Testament Church: An Extraordinary Guide to Understanding the New Testament. A detailed re-telling of the entire story of the first-century church in chronological order.

For more resources, visit our web site at **www.ptmin.org**

To obtain further information about first-century styled church life, email us at **PTMIN@aol.com**